Hamilton Beach Dual Breakfast Sandwich Maker Cookbook

Hamilton Beach Dual Breakfast Sandwich Maker Cookbook

365-Day Classic and Tasty Recipes to Enjoy Mouthwatering
Sandwiches, Burgers, Omelets and More | Healthy Cooking for
Busy People on a Budget

Wody Tonik

CONTENT

INTRODUCTION

There are so many kitchen appliances that have come out in the market over the recent years. From multi-cookers to air fryers, technology has indeed played a role in how people prepare and cook their food, making the task quicker and more convenient to suit the more hectic and fast-paced lifestyle in today's society.

It can get overwhelming finding the right kitchen appliance to invest in. If you're a sandwich lover or you find yourself constantly preparing sandwiches for your family, it's indeed a good idea to invest in a sandwich maker.

This will not only save you time but also reduce your efforts so you still have the energy to do other important tasks.

One that would certainly exceed your expectations is the incredible Hamilton Beach Dual Breakfast Sandwich Maker. This one doesn't just give you one but helps you prepare two sandwiches at the same time. It doubles your effort, cuts down your time by half!

Get to know more about what this amazing kitchen appliance can do for your cooking.

CHAPTER 1: AN OVERVIEW

What is the Hamilton Beach Dual Breakfast Sandwich Maker?

Hamilton Beach Dual Breakfast Sandwich Maker is a practical and convenient kitchen innovation that lets you prepare customized sandwiches with only four steps and in 5 minutes or less.

It's designed with practicality in mind. The setup is easy. Cleanup is no hassle. All the removable parts from the sandwich maker can be washed in your dishwasher and you don't have anything to worry about. Plus, it's safe and durable too. You can expect this device to last a very long time with you and your family. Just make sure that you follow the care tips.

Steps for Using for the First Time

Before you even start to use the sandwich maker, you must first clean it up of course. What you need to do is to lift the cover so you can remove each of the ring assembly. Wash these both using hot soapy water. Rinse thoroughly and let it dry.

Next, wipe the heating plates both top and bottom using a damp, soapy cloth. Wipe off the soap with another damp cloth and let it dry as well. The rings should be sprayed or brushed with vegetable oil before using it for the first time.

So now we get to the part where we are going to finally prepare our sandwiches using this amazing kitchen appliance.

Here are the steps to follow:

Step # 1 – Plug the wall into a socket

When you do this, the red light will turn on. Spray the rings lightly with oil. Let it preheat with the cover closed. The cooking plates should be rotated and situated in between the rings.

Step # 2 – Wait for green light to turn on

The green light will turn on to signal that the unit is heated to the right temperature.

Step # 3 – Prepare the sandwich

Add the bread slices to the sandwich maker and top it with the desired ingredients such as deli meat, cooked meat, vegetable and cheese. Make sure that you don't over fill the sandwich maker as this will cause for the food to spill.

Put down the rings and cooking plates. Crack the eggs onto the cooking plates. Don't forget to pierce the yolk using a toothpick or fork. Rotate the cooking plates so that the egg won't leak. Seal the sandwich maker and let it cook for 4 minutes.

Step # 4 – Open the sandwich maker

Use an oven mitt to open the cover. Remove the sandwich using a wooden or plastic utensil. Do not use metal. If you're going to make another sandwich, wait at least for two minutes to let the machine come to correct temperature.

Step # 5 – Unplug the sandwich maker

Do not forget this important step.

Tips

• Prepare all the ingredients needed before using the sandwich maker.
• Keep the cover sealed with the rings and cooking plates in place while you are preheating the machine.
• Check also to make sure that the rotating plates are in plates when you're adding food.

Important Safety Reminders

Although the device has been designed with safety in mind, you must still follow proper precautions to ensure that you are safe during cooking time and also so that the sandwich maker will last a long time.

Here are some important safety guidelines to heed:

1. Read all the instructions in the manual and follow everything to the dot.
2. Do not let children or people with reduced mental or physical capabilities to use the device unless supervised closely.
3. Keep the sandwich maker away from the reach of children and pets. Children should never be allowed to play with the device even when it is not plugged.
4. Never touch the hot surface with bare hands. Use the knobs or handles, and use oven mitts when opening the cover.
5. Do not submerge the plug, cord or cooking unit in water or any liquid.
6. Always unplug the socket when you're not using the device.
7. You should also make sure that it is unplugged when you are cleaning it.
8. Let it cool first before cleaning or removing any parts.
9. Do not use the device if you find any damage in the plug, cord or if you notice that the unit is malfunctioning. Call customer service to report the damage.
10. The device should not be used outdoors.
11. Make sure that the cord is not hanging over the edge of your kitchen counter or table, and that it is not anywhere near hot surfaces.
12. Do not place the sandwich maker near heated ovens or stoves.
13. Do not move the sandwich maker while it is cooking.
14. Do not use the sandwich maker for other purposes other than its intended use.
15. Do not leave the appliance unattended.
16. Place the unit in a part of your kitchen where there is enough circulation.
17. Do not use metal for removing food in the unit.
18. Let the unit cool first before putting it away.

Care & Cleaning Tips

1. To clean the unit, here are the steps to remember:
2. Unplug the unit during cooking. Let it cool first.
3. Remove the ring assemblies by holding the bottom ring handles to open them and then lift them up straight.
4. Do not use any sharp or pointed objects for cleaning.
5. Do not use any abrasive cleaners including scouring pads or steel wool for cleaning the unit.
6. Wipe the heating plates with damp soapy cloth. Remove the soap using another damp cloth. Let it dry.
7. Wipe the outside surface of the unit with damp soapy cloth.
8. If washing the parts of the unit in the dishwasher, never use the "sani" setting as this can damage the product parts.

Tips for Cooking Success

The sandwich maker does almost all the work for you, but of course, you also have to do your part to ensure that the sandwich is prepared perfectly.

Here are some important tips for cooking success:

- **Follow the recipe carefully.** The recipes in the manual and also in this book are written to ensure precise cooking. Be sure to follow the steps necessary. Do not deviate from the steps unless perfectly sure that the adjustment will work out.
- **Prepare all the ingredients first.** Do this before you preheat the machine. This will ensure that you have everything you need before you start so you can assemble the sandwich with no hassle.
- **Precook the ingredients that need to be precooked.** like meat, tofu, and other similar food. The sandwich maker will only heat the sandwich and cannot cook meat like steak strips or chicken fillets. Be sure to cook this first on your grill, oven or stove, or as specified in the recipe.
- **Use fresh and organic ingredients.** If you want quality sandwiches, then you must make sure that your ingredients are of good quality too. Choose eggs that are free range and fresh. Choose beef or pork that are lean and grass fed. The ingredients play a crucial role in the success of your sandwich making.

Troubleshooting Guide

Even topnotch kitchen devices like the Hamilton Sandwich Maker can still run into some trouble during use, especially when it is not taken care of the proper way. You can also have some problem if you are not following the steps necessary to make the device work properly.

If you encounter any of these issues, here are the solutions that you should follow:

- **Poor, slow or low heating**

  The green preheat light is a signal that the device has been heated to the correct temperature. But take note that it does not signal that the sandwich is ready. You must follow the duration for cooking specified in the recipe.

  Most sandwiches call for 4 minutes cooking. Even if the green light turns on after 3 minutes, you should wait for another minute before opening the cover of the sandwich maker and removing the sandwich from the device.

  Also, if you're going to do another batch of sandwiches, you must wait for 2 minutes before using the sandwich maker again. This will give the device enough time to reach the correct temperature.

  It's also possible that you have overfilled the sandwich maker with ingredients, which is why it is not heating properly. Reduce the amount of the ingredients if this is the case.

  Make sure that you preheat the unit with the cover closed, and with the rings and cooking plates in the correct place.

- **Undercooked eggs, under-toasted bread**

  If you are using frozen or extra large eggs, this can actually happen. This means that you need to add more cooking time. The same is true if you are using cold ingredients. Thaw the ingredients or let them come to room temperature first before cooking.

- **Overcooked eggs**

  Now it can also happen that the eggs are overcooked. With this one, you can't do anything more about it but learn from the mistake. Next time, reduce the cooking time. Take note that cooking time may possibly vary for very small eggs, egg whites and scrambled eggs.

- **Ingredients sticking to the rings or cooking plates**

Use a wooden or plastic utensil to loosen ingredients that have sticked. Next time, spray the cooking plates before preheating the device.

- **Eggs leaking from the rings**

This means that the unit has been overfilled. Do not use extra large eggs. Only large eggs can be used. You should also reduce the amount or the sizes of the ingredients that you are including in the sandwich. Do not force the cover down. If it is not closing properly normally, then it means that the unit is overfilled and there is a chance that the eggs will leak.

It's also possible that the cooking plates are not in the correct position. Check if the cooking plates are rotated to the right position.

Finally, make sure that the device is heated properly.

- **Overly browned bread**

It's possible for sugar and high fat ingredients to cause for the bread to darken too much. If this is the case, you can try cooking the eggs or other ingredients first without the bread top.

Don't worry too much if you are not able to perfect the sandwiches right away. Practice makes perfect. In no time, you will be able to create delicious sandwiches without any trouble.

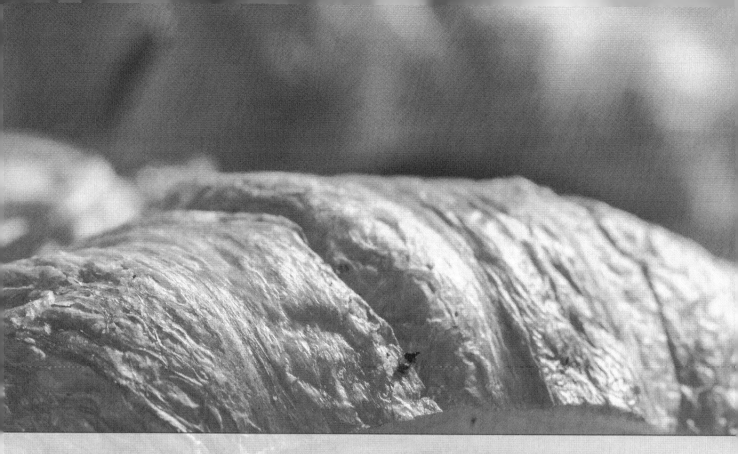

CHAPTER 2:
BREAKFAST SANDWICH RECIPES

Cheese & Egg Breakfast Sandwich

Preparation Time: 2 minutes
Cooking Time: 4 minutes
Servings: 2

Ingredients:

- 2 English muffins, split in half
- 2 slices cheese
- 2 eggs

Method:

1. Preheat your Hamilton Dual Breakfast Sandwich Maker.
2. Wait until green light turns on.
3. Open and place the bottom muffin inside.
4. Top with the cheese.
5. Place the cooking plate with ring.
6. Add the egg to the cooking plate.
7. Add the muffin top.
8. Close and cook for 4 minutes, rotating the cooking plate handle.

Serving Suggestions:

Sprinkle the egg with pepper before serving.

Preparation & Cooking Tips:

Remove using a spatula.

Apple, Egg & Cheddar Sandwich

Preparation Time: 5 minutes
Cooking Time: 4 minutes
Servings: 2

Ingredients:

- 2 croissants, sliced in half
- 4 tablespoons cheddar cheese, shredded
- 1 apple, sliced thinly
- 2 eggs

Method:

1. Preheat your Hamilton Dual Breakfast Sandwich Maker.
2. Wait until green light turns on.
3. Lift the cover.
4. Add the bottom of the croissant.
5. Top with the apple slices and cheese.
6. Place the cooking plate with top ring.
7. Add the eggs to the cooking plate.
8. Replace the croissant tops.
9. Cover and cook for 4 minutes, rotating handle.

Serving Suggestions:

Serve with coffee or hot chocolate drink.

Preparation & Cooking Tips:

Use Granny Smith apples.

Southwestern Breakfast Sandwich

Preparation Time: 5 minutes
Cooking Time: 4 minutes
Servings: 2

Ingredients:

- 2 English muffins, split in half
- ¼ avocado, sliced thinly
- 2 slices Monterey Jack cheese
- 2 eggs

Method:

1. Preheat your Hamilton Dual Breakfast Sandwich Maker.
2. Once the green light turns on, lift the cover.
3. Place the bottom muffin inside.
4. Top with the avocado and cheese.
5. Lower the cooking plate with top ring.
6. Add eggs to the cooking place.
7. Top with the muffin tops.
8. Close and cook for 4 minutes, rotating the handles.

Serving Suggestions:

Serve with tomato salsa.

Preparation & Cooking Tips:

Use whole wheat English muffins if available.

Egg & Cheese Bagel Sandwich

Preparation Time: 2 minutes
Cooking Time: 4 minutes
Servings: 2

Ingredients:

- 2 bagels, sliced in half
- 2 slices cheddar cheese
- 2 red bell pepper ring
- 2 eggs

Method:

1. Preheat your Hamilton Dual Breakfast Sandwich Maker.
2. Once the green light turns on, lift the cover.
3. Place the bottom bagel inside.
4. Top with the cheese and red bell pepper ring.
5. Lower the cooking plates with top ring.
6. Add eggs to the cooking plates.
7. Top with the bagel tops.
8. Close the lid and cook for 4 minutes, rotating the handles.

Serving Suggestions:

Serve with hot milk or chocolate.

Preparation & Cooking Tips:

You can also use orange bell pepper ring for this recipe.

Muffin with Herbed Goat Cheese, Tomato, Egg & Spinach

Preparation Time: 5 minutes
Cooking Time: 4 minutes
Servings: 2

Ingredients:

- 2 English muffins, split in half
- 2 tablespoons herbed goat cheese
- 2 slices red bell pepper ring
- 2 slices tomato
- 8 spinach leaves
- 2 eggs

Method:

1. Preheat your Hamilton Dual Breakfast Sandwich Maker.
2. Wait for the green light to turn on
3. Lift the cover.
4. Place the bottom muffin inside.
5. Top with the herbed goat cheese, red bell pepper ring, tomato and spinach.
6. Lower the cooking plates with top rings.
7. Add eggs to the cooking plates.
8. Top with the muffin tops.
9. Cover the lid.
10. Cook for 4 minutes while rotating the handles.

Serving Suggestions:

Serve with additional goat cheese.

Preparation & Cooking Tips:

Use whole wheat English muffins.

Bistro Breakfast Sandwich

Preparation Time: 10 minutes
Cooking Time: 5 minutes
Servings: 2

Ingredients:

- 4 slices sourdough bread
- 3 oz. Brie cheese, sliced thinly
- 6 bacon strips, cooked
- ½ cup baby spinach
- 8 slices apple
- 2 tablespoons melted butter
- 4 eggs

Method:

1. Preheat your Hamilton Dual Breakfast Sandwich Maker.
2. Wait for the green light to turn on.
3. Open and add the bread slices inside.
4. Top with the cheese, bacon, spinach and apple.
5. Drizzle with butter.
6. Lower the cooking plates with top rings.
7. Add eggs to the cooking plates.
8. Add the remaining bread slices.
9. Cover the lid.
10. Cook for 4 minutes while rotating the handles.

Serving Suggestions:

Serve with condiments of choice.

Preparation & Cooking Tips:

Cook bacon until crispy.

Scrambled Egg Breakfast Sandwich

Preparation Time: 5 minutes
Cooking Time: 4 minutes
Servings: 2

Ingredients:

- 4 garlic bread slices
- 6 slices mozzarella cheese
- 3 eggs, beaten
- ¼ cup milk

Method:

1. Preheat your Hamilton Dual Breakfast Sandwich Maker.
2. Once the green light turns on, lift the lid.
3. Add bread slices inside.
4. Top with the cheese.
5. In a bowl, mix the eggs and milk.
6. Lower the cooking plates with top rings.
7. Add egg mixture to the cooking plates.
8. Add the remaining bread slices.
9. Cover the lid.
10. Cook for 4 minutes while rotating the handles.

Serving Suggestions:

Season with a little salt and pepper.

Preparation & Cooking Tips:

Use part-skim mozzarella cheese if available.

Omelet Breakfast Sandwich

Preparation Time: 10 minutes
Cooking Time: 4 minutes
Servings: 2

Ingredients:

- 4 slices bread
- 4 slices cheddar cheese
- 3 eggs, beaten
- 1 red onion, minced
- 1 tomato, chopped
- 1 red bell pepper, chopped

Method:

1. Preheat your Hamilton Dual Breakfast Sandwich Maker.
2. Once the green light turns on, lift the lid.
3. Add bread slices inside.
4. Top with the cheese.
5. In a bowl, mix the eggs, red onion, tomato and bell pepper.
6. Lower the cooking plates with top rings.
7. Add egg mixture to the cooking plates.
8. Top with the remaining bread slices.
9. Cover and cook for 4 minutes, rotating the handles.

Serving Suggestions:

Serve with additional cheese slices.

Preparation & Cooking Tips:

You can also sauté first the onion, tomato and bell pepper in a pan before using.

Egg & Sausage Breakfast Sandwich

Preparation Time: 10 minutes
Cooking Time: 4 minutes
Servings: 2

Ingredients:

- 1 teaspoon olive oil
- 4 links pork sausage, removed from casing and crumbled
- 1 tablespoon white onion, chopped
- 2 eggs, beaten
- 4 slices whole wheat bread

Method:

1. In a pan over medium heat, add the olive oil and cook sausage until browned.
2. Drain fat.
3. Mix the eggs and crumbled cooked sausage.
4. Preheat your Hamilton Dual Breakfast Sandwich Maker.
5. Once the green light turns on, lift the lid.
6. Place the bread slices inside.
7. Lower the cooking plates with top rings.
8. Add egg mixture to the cooking plates.
9. Top with the remaining bread slices.
10. Cover and cook for 4 minutes, rotating the handles.

Serving Suggestions:

Serve with tomato salad.

Preparation & Cooking Tips:

You can also use other types of sausage for this recipe.

Egg & Spinach Sandwich

Preparation Time: 5 minutes
Cooking Time: 4 minutes
Servings: 4

Ingredients:

- 8 slices whole wheat bread
- 1 tablespoon cheddar cheese, shredded
- 8 spinach leaves
- 4 eggs

Method:

1. Preheat your Hamilton Dual Breakfast Sandwich Maker.
2. Wait for the green light to turn on.
3. Open and add bread slices inside.
4. Top with the cheese and spinach.
5. Lower the cooking plates with top rings.
6. Add eggs to the cooking plates.
7. Top with the remaining bread slices.
8. Cover and cook for 4 minutes, rotating the handles.

Serving Suggestions:

Serve with salsa.

Preparation & Cooking Tips:

You can also use English muffin for this recipe.

Italian Sausage Breakfast Sandwich

Preparation Time: 10 minutes
Cooking Time: 4 minutes
Servings: 2

Ingredients:

- 1 teaspoon olive oil
- 4 Italian sausage links, removed from casing and crumbled
- 4 bread slices
- ½ cup cheddar cheese, shredded
- 2 eggs, beaten
- ½ red onion, minced
- ½ tomato, chopped

Method:

1. Add the olive oil to a pan over medium heat.
2. Cook Italian sausage until browned.
3. Drain fat.
4. In a bowl, combine eggs, onion, tomato and crumbled cooked sausage.
5. Preheat your Hamilton Dual Breakfast Sandwich Maker.
6. Once the green light turns on, lift the cover.
7. Add bread slices inside.
8. Lower the cooking plates with top rings.
9. Add egg mixture to the cooking plates.
10. Top with the remaining bread slices.
11. Cover and cook for 4 minutes, rotating the handles.

Serving Suggestions:
Serve with hot pepper sauce or mustard.

Preparation & Cooking Tips:
You can also add chopped bell pepper to the egg mixture.

Ham, Egg & Cheese Breakfast Sandwich

Preparation Time: 2 minutes
Cooking Time: 4 minutes
Servings: 2

Ingredients:

- 2 slices ham
- 2 slices cheddar cheese
- 2 eggs
- 4 bread slices

Method:

1.Preheat your Hamilton Dual Breakfast Sandwich Maker.
2.Wait until green light turns on.
3.Open and place the bread slices inside.
4.Top with ham and cheddar cheese.
5.Place the cooking plates with ring.
6.Add the eggs to the cooking plate.
7.Add the remaining bread slices.
8.Close and cook for 4 minutes, rotating the cooking plate handle.

Serving Suggestions:

Serve with hash browns.

Preparation & Cooking Tips:

You can also use chicken ham to lower fat and calorie content of this sandwich.

Spanish Style Breakfast Sandwich

Preparation Time: 5 minutes
Cooking Time: 4 minutes
Servings: 2

Ingredients:

- 4 bread slices
- 1 tablespoon Manchego cheese, shredded
- 3 eggs, beaten
- 1 tablespoon roasted sweet red pepper, chopped
- 1 tablespoon green onion, chopped
- 2 teaspoons fresh oregano, minced

Method:

1. Preheat your Hamilton Dual Breakfast Sandwich Maker.
2. Wait for the green light to turn on.
3. Open and add bread slices inside.
4. Mix the remaining ingredients in a bowl.
5. Lower the cooking plates with top rings.
6. Add egg mixture to the cooking plates.
7. Top with the remaining bread slices.
8. Seal and cook for 4 minutes, rotating the handles.

Serving Suggestions:

Serve with fresh fruits.

Preparation & Cooking Tips:

Use cheddar cheese if Manchego cheese is not available.

Breakfast Biscuit Sandwich

Preparation Time: 2 minutes
Cooking Time: 4 minutes
Servings: 2

Ingredients:

- 4 frozen biscuits
- 2 teaspoons butter
- 4 slices process cheese
- 4 slices deli ham
- 4 eggs

Method:

1. Preheat your Hamilton Dual Breakfast Sandwich Maker.
2. Wait for the green light to turn on.
3. Lift the lid up.
4. Add biscuits inside.
5. Top with the cheese and ham.
6. Lower the cooking plates with top rings.
7. Add eggs to the cooking plates.
8. Top with the remaining biscuits.
9. Cover and cook for 4 minutes, rotating the handles.

Serving Suggestions:

Drizzle with a little butter before serving.

Preparation & Cooking Tips:

Thaw the frozen biscuit first before using.

Waffle Sandwiches

Preparation Time: 2 minutes
Cooking Time: 4 minutes
Servings: 2

Ingredients:

- 4 frozen waffles
- ¼ cup hazelnut spread
- 1 banana, sliced

Method:

1. Preheat your Hamilton Dual Breakfast Sandwich Maker.
2. Once the green light turns on, lift the lid.
3. Add the waffles inside.
4. Spread with the hazelnut spread and banana.
5. Top with remaining waffles.
6. Cover and cook for 4 minutes.

Serving Suggestions:

Serve with additional hazelnut spread.

Preparation & Cooking Tips:

You can also use peanut butter if hazelnut spread is not available.

Green Egg & Ham Breakfast Sandwich

Preparation Time: 5 minutes
Cooking Time: 4 minutes
Servings: 2

Ingredients:

- 4 English muffins, split in half
- 2 slices deli ham
- 2 slices provolone cheese
- 2 eggs, beaten
- 3 tablespoons pesto
- 1/8 cup milk

Method:

1. Preheat your Hamilton Dual Breakfast Sandwich Maker.
2. Wait for the green light to turn on.
3. Open and add muffin bottoms inside.
4. Top with ham and cheese.
5. Mix the remaining ingredients in a bowl.
6. Lower the cooking plates with top rings.
7. Add egg mixture to the cooking plates.
8. Top with the muffin tops.
9. Cover and cook for 4 minutes, rotating the handles.

Serving Suggestions:

Serve with additional pesto.

Preparation & Cooking Tips:

Use nonfat milk and low fat cheese.

French Toast Sandwich

Preparation Time: 5 minutes
Cooking Time: 5 minutes
Servings: 2

Ingredients:

- 4 slices bread
- ¼ cup orange marmalade
- ¼ cup cream cheese
- 2 eggs, beaten
- 2 tablespoons milk
- 1 teaspoon sugar

Method:

1. Preheat your Hamilton Dual Breakfast Sandwich Maker.
2. Wait for the green light to turn on.
3. Open and add bread slices inside.
4. Spread orange marmalade and cream cheese on top.
5. Top with remaining bread slices.
6. Cover and cook for 2 minutes.
7. Lift the cover.
8. Mix the eggs, milk and sugar.
9. Dip sandwich in the egg mixture.
10. Cook in the sandwich maker for another 3 minutes.

Serving Suggestions:

Serve with maple syrup.

Preparation & Cooking Tips:

Use day-old bread for this recipe.

Tex-Mex Breakfast Sandwich

Preparation Time: 7 minutes
Cooking Time: 4 minutes
Servings: 4

Ingredients:

- 1 tablespoon olive oil
- 1 red onion, chopped
- 1 red bell pepper, chopped
- 1 jalapeno pepper, chopped
- ½ cup mushrooms, sliced
- 4 eggs, beaten
- ¼ cup Mexican cheese blend, shredded
- 8 bread slices

Method:

1. Add olive oil to a pan over medium heat.
2. Cook the onion, peppers and mushrooms.
3. Add the eggs to a bowl.
4. Stir in the onion mixture.
5. Preheat your Hamilton Dual Breakfast Sandwich Maker.
6. Wait for the green light to turn on.
7. Open and add bread slices inside.
8. Top with cheese.
9. Lower the cooking plates and top rings.
10. Add the egg mixture to the cooking plates.
11. Add remaining bread slices on top.
12. Cover and cook for 4 minutes, rotating handles.

Serving Suggestions:

Serve with sour cream, hot pepper sauce, and guacamole.

Preparation & Cooking Tips:

Use cheddar cheese if Mexican cheese blend is not available.

Scrambled Egg & Salsa Sandwiches

Preparation Time: 5 minutes
Cooking Time: 4 minutes
Servings: 2

Ingredients:

- 4 slices bread
- ½ cup cheddar cheese, shredded
- 3 eggs
- ½ cup salsa

Method:

1. Preheat your Hamilton Dual Breakfast Sandwich Maker.
2. Wait for the green light to turn on.
3. Open and add bread slices inside.
4. Top with cheese.
5. Mix eggs and salsa in a bowl.
6. Lower the cooking plates with top rings.
7. Add egg mixture to the cooking plates.
8. Top with the remaining bread slices.
9. Cover and cook for 4 minutes, rotating the handles.

Serving Suggestions:

Serve with avocado slices.

Preparation & Cooking Tips:

You can use either homemade or prepared salsa for this recipe.

Bacon, Egg & Cheese Breakfast Sandwich

Preparation Time: 5 minutes
Cooking Time: 4 minutes
Servings: 2

Ingredients:

- 4 bread slices
- 4 slices bacon, cooked crisp
- 4 slices cheese
- 2 eggs

Method:

1. Preheat your Hamilton Dual Breakfast Sandwich Maker.
2. Wait for the green light to turn on.
3. Lift the lid up.
4. Add bread slices inside.
5. Top with bacon and cheese.
6. Lower the cooking plates with top rings.
7. Add eggs to the cooking plates.
8. Top with the remaining bread slices.
9. Seal the sandwich maker.
10. Cook for 4 minutes, rotating the handles.

Serving Suggestions:

Serve with coffee or hot chocolate drink.

Preparation & Cooking Tips:

Use low fat cheese.

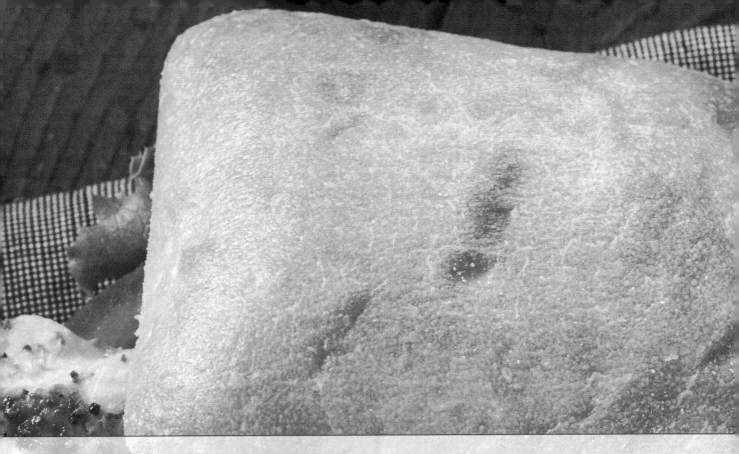

CHAPTER 3:
CHICKEN SANDWICH RECIPES

Chicken & Swiss Cheese Sandwich

Preparation Time: 15 minutes
Cooking Time: 4 minutes
Servings: 4

Ingredients:

- 8 slices bread
- 4 chicken breast fillet
- Salt and pepper to taste
- 1 teaspoon dried oregano
- 1 egg, beaten
- ¼ cup breadcrumbs
- 2 tablespoons olive oil
- 4 strips bacon, cooked crisp and sliced in half
- 4 slices Swiss cheese

Method:

1. Season chicken breast with salt and pepper.
2. Dip in egg and dredge with breadcrumbs.
3. Add olive oil to a pan over medium heat.
4. Cook chicken until crispy.
5. Preheat your Hamilton Dual Breakfast Sandwich Maker.
6. Wait for the green light to turn on.
7. Open and add the bread slices inside.
8. Top with chicken, bacon and Swiss cheese.
9. Add remaining bread slices.
10. Seal the sandwich maker.
11. Cook for 4 minutes.

Serving Suggestions:

Add lettuce and tomato to the sandwich before serving.

Preparation & Cooking Tips:

You can also use frozen breaded chicken fillet for this recipe.

Sweet & Spicy Chicken Sandwich

Preparation Time: 15 minutes
Cooking Time: 4 minutes
Servings: 2

Ingredients:

- 2 chicken breast fillets
- Salt and pepper to taste
- 2 tablespoons olive oil
- ¼ cup ketchup
- ¼ cup sweet chili sauce
- 1 teaspoon lime juice
- 1 teaspoon ground ginger
- 2 cloves garlic, minced
- Pepper to taste
- 2 English muffins, sliced in half
- 2 slices mozzarella cheese

Method:

1. Season chicken with salt and pepper.
2. Add olive oil to a pan over medium heat.
3. Cook chicken until browned.
4. Mix the ketchup, chili sauce, lime juice, ginger, garlic and pepper in a bowl.
5. Dip chicken in the sauce mixture.
6. Preheat your Hamilton Dual Breakfast Sandwich Maker.
7. Wait for the green light to turn on.
8. Open and add the bread slices inside.
9. Top with chicken with sauce.
10. Add remaining bread slices.
11. Cover and cook for 4 minutes.

Serving Suggestions:

Serve with potato fries.

Preparation & Cooking Tips:

Use low fat mozzarella cheese.

Grilled Chicken Sandwich with Cheese

Preparation Time: 10 minutes
Cooking Time: 10 minutes
Servings: 2

Ingredients:

- 2 chicken breast fillet
- 1 teaspoon olive oil
- Salt and pepper to taste
- 4 slices Italian bread
- 4 slices Swiss cheese

Method:

1. Preheat your grill to medium.
2. Drizzle chicken with olive oil.
3. Season with salt and pepper.
4. Grill chicken until fully cooked.
5. Preheat your Hamilton Dual Breakfast Sandwich Maker.
6. Wait for the green light to turn on.
7. Once green light is on, open and add the bread slices inside.
8. Top with chicken and cheese.
9. Add remaining bread slices.
10. Cover and cook for 4 minutes.

Serving Suggestions:

Add shredded lettuce and tomato slices in the sandwich before serving.

Preparation & Cooking Tips:

You can also use mozzarella cheese.

Indian Chicken Sandwich

Preparation Time: 10 minutes
Cooking Time: 15 minutes
Servings: 2

Ingredients:

- 2 chicken breast fillet
- Garlic powder to taste
- 1 teaspoon paprika
- ¼ teaspoon ground turmeric
- ½ teaspoon cayenne pepper
- 2 tablespoons olive oil
- 2 teaspoons butter, softened
- 4 whole wheat bread slices

Method:

1. Season chicken with spices.
2. Add the olive oil to a pan over medium heat.
3. Cook chicken for 3 to 5 minutes per side or until fully cooked.
4. Preheat your Hamilton Dual Breakfast Sandwich Maker.
5. Wait for the green light to turn on.
6. Once green light is on, open and add the bread slices inside.
7. Spread butter on top of the bread.
8. Add chicken on top.
9. Add remaining bread slices.
10. Cover and cook for 4 minutes.

Serving Suggestions:

Add baby spinach to the sandwich.

Preparation & Cooking Tips:

You can also use a slow cooker to cook the chicken but add 1 cup chicken broth to the pot.

Chicken & Blackberry Sandwich

Preparation Time: 40 minutes
Cooking Time: 15 minutes
Servings: 2

Ingredients:

- ¼ cup balsamic vinegar
- 2 tablespoons molasses
- ¼ cup sweet chili sauce
- 1 tablespoon Dijon mustard
- Salt and pepper to taste
- 2 chicken breast fillets
- 2 tablespoons olive oil
- 2 English muffins, split in half
- 1 cup blackberry jam

Method:

1. Mix the vinegar, molasses, sweet chili sauce, mustard, salt and pepper.
2. Add chicken to the marinade.
3. Marinate for 30 minutes.
4. Add olive oil to a pan over medium heat.
5. Cook chicken for 3 to 5 minutes per side.
6. Preheat your Hamilton Dual Breakfast Sandwich Maker.
7. Wait for the green light to turn on.
8. Once green light is on, open and add the muffin bottoms inside.
9. Spread blackberry jam on top of the bread.
10. Add chicken on top.
11. Add muffin tops.
12. Cover and cook for 4 minutes.

Serving Suggestions:

Serve with fresh green salad.

Preparation & Cooking Tips:

You can also use blueberry jam for this recipe.

Chicken Parmesan Sandwich

Preparation Time: 15 minutes
Cooking Time: 15 minutes
Servings: 4

Ingredients:

- 4 chicken breast fillets
- Salt and pepper to taste
- 1 egg, beaten
- 1/8 cup Parmesan cheese
- 1/8 cup breadcrumbs
- 2 tablespoons olive oil
- 8 slices whole wheat bread
- 1 cup marinara sauce
- 4 slices Provolone cheese

Method:

1. Season chicken with salt and pepper.
2. Dip in egg.
3. Dredge with Parmesan cheese and breadcrumbs.
4. Add olive oil to a pan over medium heat.
5. Cook chicken for 3 to 5 minutes per side.
6. Preheat your Hamilton Dual Breakfast Sandwich Maker.
7. Wait for the green light to turn on.
8. Once green light is on, open and add the bread slices inside.
9. Spread marinara sauce on top of the bread.
10. Add chicken on top.
11. Add remaining bread slices.
12. Cover and cook for 4 minutes.

Serving Suggestions:
Garnish with fresh basil leaves.

Preparation & Cooking Tips:
You can add dried oregano and rosemary to the marinara sauce.

Chicken with Lemon Dill Spread

Preparation Time: 15 minutes
Cooking Time: 9 minutes
Servings: 2

Ingredients:

- 3 tablespoons butter
- 1 clove garlic, minced
- 2 chicken breast fillets
- 4 slices French bread
- ¼ cup cream cheese, softened
- 1 teaspoon lemon juice
- ½ teaspoon dill weed

Method:

1. Add butter to a pan over medium heat.
2. Cook the garlic for 30 seconds, stirring often.
3. Add the chicken and cook for 3 to 5 minutes per side.
4. Transfer to a plate.
5. Preheat your Hamilton Dual Breakfast Sandwich Maker.
6. Wait for the green light to turn on.
7. Once green light is on, open and add the French bread slices inside.
8. In a bowl, mix the remaining ingredients.
9. Spread cream cheese mixture on top of the bread slices.
10. Add chicken on top.
11. Add remaining bread slices.
12. Cover and cook for 4 minutes.

Serving Suggestions:

Add lettuce and tomato slices to the sandwich.

Preparation & Cooking Tips:

Flatten chicken before seasoning.

Chicken in Biscuit Sandwich

Preparation Time: 10 minutes
Cooking Time: 15 minutes
Servings: 2

Ingredients:

- 2 chicken breast fillets
- Salt and pepper to taste
- 2 tablespoons olive oil
- 2 buttermilk biscuits, sliced in half
- 4 tablespoons cranberry jam

Method:

1. Season chicken with salt and pepper.
2. Add olive oil to a pan over medium heat.
3. Cook chicken for 3 to 5 minutes per side.
4. Preheat your Hamilton Dual Breakfast Sandwich Maker.
5. Wait for the green light to turn on.
6. Once green light is on, open and add the biscuits inside.
7. Spread cranberry jam on top of the bread slices.
8. Add chicken on top.
9. Add remaining bread slices.
10. Cover and cook for 4 minutes.

Serving Suggestions:

Add thinly sliced red onion rings to the sandwich before serving.

Preparation & Cooking Tips:

You can also use frozen breaded chicken for this recipe.

Pulled Chicken Sandwich

Preparation Time: 15 minutes
Cooking Time: 4 hours and 4 minutes

Ingredients:

Servings: 6
- ¼ cup chicken broth
- 1 onion, chopped
- 2 cloves garlic, minced
- 6 oz. tomato paste
- 1 tablespoon cider vinegar
- 2 tablespoons brown sugar
- 1 tablespoon Worcestershire sauce
- 1 tablespoon yellow mustard
- 2 teaspoons chili powder
- Salt to taste
- 1 ½ lb. chicken breast fillet
- 6 burger buns, split in half

Method:

1. Add all ingredients except buns inside the slow cooker.
2. Mix well.
3. Cover and cook on low for 4 hours.
4. Shred chicken with forks.
5. Preheat your Hamilton Dual Breakfast Sandwich Maker.
6. Wait for the green light to turn on.
7. Once green light is on, open and add the bread slices inside.
8. Top with the pulled chicken and a little cooking liquid.
9. Add remaining bread slices.
10. Cover and cook for 4 minutes.

Serving Suggestions:

Add lettuce to the sandwich.

Preparation & Cooking Tips:

Use reduced-sodium chicken broth.

Lime Chicken Sandwich

Preparation Time: 15 minutes
Cooking Time: 15 minutes
Servings: 2

Ingredients:

- 2 chicken breast fillets
- 2 tablespoons lime juice
- 1 teaspoon ground cumin
- Salt and pepper to taste
- 2 tablespoons olive oil
- 2 English muffins, sliced in half
- 4 tablespoons cream cheese

Method:

1. Drizzle chicken with lime juice.
2. Season with cumin, salt and pepper.
3. Add olive oil to a pan over medium heat.
4. Cook chicken for 3 to 5 minutes per side.
5. Preheat your Hamilton Dual Breakfast Sandwich Maker.
6. Wait for the green light to turn on.
7. Lift the cover.
8. Add the muffin bottoms inside.
9. Spread with cream cheese.
10. Top with chicken.
11. Add muffin tops.
12. Cover and cook for 4 minutes.

Serving Suggestions:

Add thinly sliced avocado to the sandwich.

Preparation & Cooking Tips:

You can also use chicken thigh fillets.

CHAPTER 4:
BEEF SANDWICH RECIPES

Steak Sandwich

Preparation Time: 15 minutes
Cooking Time: 15 minutes
Servings: 2

Ingredients:

- 1 top sirloin steak
- 1 teaspoon steak seasoning
- 1 tablespoon olive oil
- 1 tablespoon butter
- 2 English muffins, split
- 1 tablespoon mayo

Method:

1. Season steak with steak seasoning.
2. Add olive oil and butter to a pan over medium heat.
3. Cook steak for 3 to 5 minutes per side.
4. Transfer to a cutting board and slice into strips.
5. Preheat your Hamilton Dual Breakfast Sandwich Maker.
6. Wait for the green light to turn on.
7. Lift the cover.
8. Add the muffin bottoms inside.
9. Spread with mayo.
10. Top with steak strips.
11. Add muffin tops.
12. Cover and cook for 4 minutes.

Serving Suggestions:

Add fresh arugula and tomato slices to the sandwich.

Preparation & Cooking Tips:

You can also add caramelized onions to the sandwich if you like.

Lebanese Street Sandwich

Preparation Time: 15 minutes
Cooking Time: 15 minutes
Servings: 6

Ingredients:

- 2 white onion, chopped
- 1 ½ cups parsley
- 1 egg, beaten
- 1 ½ lb. ground beef
- Salt to taste
- 1 tablespoon olive oil
- 12 whole wheat bread slices
- 2 tablespoons olive oil
- 1/3 cup tahini
- ¼ cup lemon juice
- 2 cloves garlic, minced
- 2 tablespoons water

Method:

1. Add onion and parsley to a food processor.
2. Process until smooth.
3. Transfer to a bowl.
4. Stir in the egg, ground beef and salt.
5. Shape into patties.
6. Add olive oil to a pan over medium heat.
7. Cook until browned on both sides.
8. Mix the remaining ingredients except bread in a bowl.
9. Preheat your Hamilton Dual Breakfast Sandwich Maker.
10. Wait for the green light to turn on.
11. Lift the cover.
12. Add the bread slices inside.
13. Spread with sauce mixture.
14. Top with beef patties.
15. Add remaining bread slices.
16. Cover and cook for 4 minutes.

Serving Suggestions: Serve with additional sauce.

Preparation & Cooking Tips: Use lean ground beef.

Beef & Mushroom Burgers

Preparation Time: 15 minutes
Cooking Time: 15 minutes
Servings: 2

Ingredients:

- 1 lb. ground beef
- 1 cup mushrooms, chopped
- 1 red onion, minced
- 1 bell pepper, minced
- 1 egg, beaten
- 1 tablespoon breadcrumbs
- 2 burger buns, split

Method:

1. Combine all the ingredients except buns in a bowl.
2. Shape into patties.
3. Cook patties in a pan over medium heat until browned on both sides.
4. Preheat your Hamilton Dual Breakfast Sandwich Maker.
5. Wait for the green light to turn on.
6. Open and add bun bottoms inside.
7. Top with beef patties.
8. Add bun tops.
9. Cover and cook for 4 minutes.

Serving Suggestions:

Serve with pickles, tomato slices and lettuce.

Preparation & Cooking Tips:

You can also spread bread mayo on top of bun bottoms before adding burger.

Mexican Beef Sandwich

Preparation Time: 15 minutes
Cooking Time: 15 minutes
Servings: 2

Ingredients:

- 2 sirloin steaks
- Salt and pepper to taste
- 1 teaspoon olive oil
- 1 red bell pepper, sliced into strips
- 1 white onion, sliced into strips
- 1 teaspoon taco seasoning
- 2 tablespoons cream cheese
- 4 whole wheat bread slices

Method:

1. Preheat your grill to medium.
2. Season steaks with salt and pepper.
3. Grill for 3 to 5 minutes per side or until well done.
4. Transfer to a cutting board.
5. Slice into strips.
6. Add olive oil to a pan over medium heat.
7. Cook red bell pepper, white onion and steak strips for 1 minute, stirring often.
8. Season with taco seasoning.
9. Preheat your Hamilton Dual Breakfast Sandwich Maker.
10. Wait for the green light to turn on.
11. Open and add bread slices inside.
12. Top with beef mixture.
13. Add remaining bread slices.
14. Cover and cook for 4 minutes.

Serving Suggestions:

Serve with salsa.

Preparation & Cooking Tips:

You can also use strip steak for this recipe.

Roast Beef & Cheese Sandwich

Preparation Time: 2 minutes
Cooking Time: 4 minutes
Servings: 2

Ingredients:

- 2 English muffins, split
- 4 slices deli roast beef
- 4 slices provolone cheese

Method:

1. Preheat your Hamilton Dual Breakfast Sandwich Maker.
2. Wait for the green light to turn on.
3. Lift the lid.
4. Add muffins inside.
5. Top with beef and cheese.
6. Add remaining bread slices.
7. Seal the sandwich maker.
8. Cook for 4 minutes.

Serving Suggestions:

Add sweet red pepper rings to your sandwich.

Preparation & Cooking Tips:

Serve with your favorite condiments.

Bacon Cheeseburger

Preparation Time: 15 minutes
Cooking Time: 10 minutes
Servings: 3

Ingredients:

Patty
- 1 lb. ground beef
- 1 clove garlic, minced
- 1 teaspoon Worcestershire sauce
- Salt and pepper to taste

Burger
- 4 burger buns, split in half
- ¼ cup mayonnaise
- 2 tablespoons ketchup
- 8 slices bacon, cooked
- 4 slices cheddar cheese

Method:
1. Preheat your grill.
2. Mix the patty ingredients in a bowl.
3. Shape into patties.
4. Grill for 3 minutes per side.
5. Preheat your Hamilton Dual Breakfast Sandwich Maker.
6. Once the green light is on, open the lid.
7. Add buns inside.
8. Spread with mayo and ketchup.
9. Top with patty, bacon and cheese.
10. Add remaining buns.
11. Seal the sandwich maker.
12. Cook for 4 minutes.

Serving Suggestions:
Add lettuce and tomato.

Preparation & Cooking Tips:
You can also add a tablespoon of breadcrumbs to the patty mixture.

Cuban Sandwich

Preparation Time: 10 minutes
Cooking Time: 10 minutes
Servings: 4

Ingredients:

Patty
- ½ lb. ground beef
- ½ lb. ground pork
- 1 tablespoon lemon juice
- Garlic salt and pepper to taste

Sandwich
- ½ cup mayonnaise
- ¼ cup Dijon mustard
- 8 slices whole wheat bread
- 8 slices Swiss cheese
- 4 slices deli ham

Method:

1. Mix patty ingredients in a bowl.
2. Shape into patties.
3. In another bowl, mix mayo and mustard.
4. Grill or fry patties for 3 minutes per side.
5. Preheat your Hamilton Dual Breakfast Sandwich Maker.
6. Wait for the green light to turn on.
7. Lift the lid.
8. Add bread slices inside.
9. Spread with mayo mixture.
10. Top with beef patty, deli ham and cheese.
11. Add remaining bread slices.
12. Close the sandwich maker.
13. Cook for 4 minutes.

Serving Suggestions:

Add pickles to your sandwich before serving.

Preparation & Cooking Tips:

You can also use burger buns for this recipe.

Beef & Onion Sandwich

Preparation Time: 15 minutes
Cooking Time: 15 minutes
Servings: 2

Ingredients:

- 1 tablespoon olive oil
- 1 white onion, sliced into rings
- 4 whole wheat bread slices
- 2 sirloin steaks, grilled and sliced into strips
- 2 slices Swiss cheese

Method:

1. Add olive oil to a pan over medium low heat.
2. Cook the onion rings for 5 to 10 minutes, stirring often.
3. Preheat your Hamilton Dual Breakfast Sandwich Maker.
4. Wait for the green light to turn on.
5. Open the sandwich maker.
6. Add bread slices inside.
7. Top with beef strips, onion rings and cheese.
8. Add remaining bread slices.
9. Seal the sandwich maker.
10. Cook for 4 minutes.

Serving Suggestions:

Serve with hot pepper sauce.

Preparation & Cooking Tips:

You can also use mozzarella cheese.

Beef & Green Chili Sandwich

Preparation Time: 15 minutes
Cooking Time: 6 minutes
Servings: 2

Ingredients:

- 1 tablespoon olive oil
- 2 green chili
- 4 whole wheat bread slices
- 2 sirloin steaks, grilled and sliced into strips
- 2 slices cheddar cheese

Method:

1. Add olive oil to a pan over medium heat.
2. Cook the green chili for 1 minute per side.
3. Transfer to a cutting board and slice into rings.
4. Preheat your Hamilton Dual Breakfast Sandwich Maker.
5. When the green light is on, lift the cover.
6. Add bread slices inside.
7. Top with beef strips, chili rings and cheese.
8. Add remaining bread slices.
9. Close the cover and cook for 4 minutes.

Serving Suggestions:

Serve with favorite condiments.

Preparation & Cooking Tips:

Use gloves when slicing green chili.

Cheesy Meatball Sandwich

Preparation Time: 20 minutes
Cooking Time: 15 minutes
Servings: 4

Ingredients:

Meatball
- 1 lb. ground beef
- ¼ cup breadcrumbs
- 1 egg, beaten
- ½ teaspoon dried oregano
- 3 cloves garlic, minced
- 1 teaspoon Italian seasoning
- ½ teaspoon red pepper flakes

Sandwich
- 2 tablespoons olive oil
- 4 English muffins, sliced in half
- 4 slices mozzarella cheese

Method:

1. Combine meatball ingredients in a bowl.
2. Form balls from the mixture.
3. Add olive oil to a pan over medium heat.
4. Cook meatballs until browned on all sides.
5. Preheat your Hamilton Dual Breakfast Sandwich Maker.
6. Once the green light is on, open the cover.
7. Add bread slices inside.
8. Top with meatballs and cheese.
9. Add remaining bread slices.
10. Seal and cook for 4 minutes.

Serving Suggestions:
Serve with pasta.

Preparation & Cooking Tips:
Use lean ground beef.

CHAPTER 5:
PORK SANDWICH RECIPES

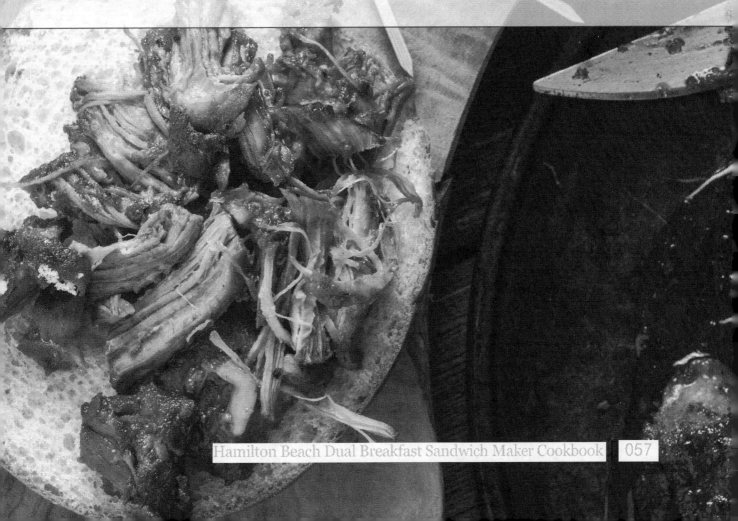

Ham & Mustard Sandwich

Preparation Time: 5 minutes
Cooking Time: 4 minutes
Servings: 2

Ingredients:

- 2 tablespoons mustard
- 1 tablespoon butter
- 2 tablespoons ketchup
- 2 slices deli ham
- 4 whole wheat bread slices

Method:

1. Mix mustard, butter and ketchup in a bowl.
2. Preheat your Hamilton Dual Breakfast Sandwich Maker.
3. When the green light is on, lift the cover.
4. Add whole wheat bread slices inside.
5. Spread with mustard mixture and top with ham.
6. Add remaining bread slices.
7. Cover the sandwich maker.
8. Cook for 4 minutes.

Serving Suggestions:

Add fresh arugula to the sandwich.

Preparation & Cooking Tips:

You can also add cheese slices if you like.

Maple & Barbecue Ham Sandwich

Preparation Time: 5 minutes
Cooking Time: 4 minutes
Servings: 2

Ingredients:

- 2 tablespoons maple syrup
- 3 tablespoons barbecue sauce
- 1 tablespoon Dijon mustard
- 4 whole wheat bread slices
- 2 deli ham slices

Method:

1. Mix maple syrup, barbecue sauce and mustard.
2. Preheat your Hamilton Dual Breakfast Sandwich Maker.
3. Wait for the green light to turn on.
4. Open the sandwich maker.
5. Add whole wheat bread slices inside.
6. Spread with maple sauce mixture.
7. Top with ham.
8. Brush ham with the sauce mixture as well.
9. Add remaining bread slices.
10. Cover the sandwich maker.
11. Cook for 4 minutes.

Serving Suggestions:

Serve with cucumber salad.

Preparation & Cooking Tips:

You can also use pulled pork for this recipe.

Basil Pork Burger

Preparation Time: 15 minutes
Cooking Time: 15 minutes
Servings: 4

Ingredients:

Patty
- 1 lb. ground pork
- 1 tablespoon breadcrumbs
- ½ red onion, minced
- 1 tablespoon fresh basil, chopped
- Salt and pepper to taste

Burger
- 1 tablespoon olive oil
- ¼ cup barbecue sauce
- 2 tablespoons mayo
- 4 burger buns

Method:

1. Combine patty ingredients in a bowl.
2. Shape into patties.
3. Add olive oil to a pan over medium heat.
4. Cook patties for 3 to 5 minutes per side.
5. Preheat your Hamilton Dual Breakfast Sandwich Maker.
6. Wait for the green light to turn on.
7. Lift the lid.
8. Add burger bun bottoms inside.
9. Spread with mixture of barbecue sauce and mayo.
10. Top with cooked patties.
11. Add tops of burger buns.
12. Cover the sandwich maker.
13. Cook for 4 minutes.

Serving Suggestions:

Serve with additional barbecue sauce.

Preparation & Cooking Tips:

You can also make the patty with a mix of ground pork and ground beef.

Ham, Cheese & Pickles Sandwich

Preparation Time: 5 minutes
Cooking Time: 4 minutes
Servings: 2

Ingredients:

- 4 whole wheat bread slices
- 4 tablespoons mayonnaise
- 2 deli ham slices
- 2 slices cheddar or Swiss cheese
- 4 slices sweet pickles

Method:

1. Preheat your Hamilton Dual Breakfast Sandwich Maker.
2. Wait for the green light to turn on.
3. Uncover the sandwich maker.
4. Add whole wheat bread slices inside.
5. Spread with mayo.
6. Top with ham, cheese and pickles.
7. Add remaining bread slices.
8. Cover the sandwich maker.
9. Cook for 4 minutes.

Serving Suggestions:

Serve with mustard and ketchup.

Preparation & Cooking Tips:

You can also use burger buns for this sandwich.

Caribbean Pork Sandwich

Preparation Time: 30 minutes
Cooking Time: 8 hours and 4 minutes
Servings: 4

Method:

1. Combine pulled pork ingredients in your slow cooker.
2. Cover and cook on low for 8 hours.
3. Transfer pork to a cutting board.
4. Shred pork with a fork.
5. Mix mayo and cilantro in a bowl.
6. Preheat your Hamilton Dual Breakfast Sandwich Maker.
7. Wait for the green light to turn on.
8. Open the sandwich maker.
9. Add burger bottoms inside.
10. Spread with mayo mixture.
11. Top with pulled pork.
12. Add burger tops.
13. Cover the sandwich maker.
14. Cook for 4 minutes.

Ingredients:

Pulled pork

- 1 pork shoulder roast (boneless)
- 1 onion, sliced
- 5 cloves garlic, minced
- ¼ cup brown sugar
- 2 cups chicken broth
- 3 teaspoons chipotle peppers in adobo sauce, minced
- 2 tablespoons ground cumin
- Salt and pepper to taste

Sandwich

- 4 tablespoons mayonnaise
- 1 tablespoon cilantro, chopped
- 4 burger buns

Serving Suggestions:

Add pineapple slice to the sandwich before serving.

Preparation & Cooking Tips:

Use low-sodium chicken broth.

Peanut Pork Sandwich

Preparation Time: 5 minutes
Cooking Time: 7 minutes
Servings: 2

Ingredients:

- 4 tablespoon peanut butter
- 1 teaspoon sweet chili sauce
- 1 teaspoon curry powder
- 2 tablespoons cooked pulled pork
- 4 whole wheat bread slices

Method:

1. Combine peanut butter, chili sauce and curry powder in a pan over medium heat.
2. Stir in the pulled pork.
3. Heat through for 3 minutes, stirring.
4. Preheat your Hamilton Dual Breakfast Sandwich Maker.
5. Wait for the green light to turn on.
6. Lift the cover.
7. Add bread slices inside.
8. Top with pulled pork mixture.
9. Add remaining bread slices.
10. Cover the sandwich maker.
11. Cook for 4 minutes.

Serving Suggestions:

Add basil leaves to the sandwich.

Preparation & Cooking Tips:

Use creamy peanut butter.

Hawaiian Pulled Pork Sandwich

Preparation Time: 30 minutes
Cooking Time: 8 hours and 4 minutes
Servings: 4

Ingredients:

- 1 pork shoulder roast (boneless)
- 1 teaspoon rubbed sage
- 1 teaspoon ground ginger
- Salt and pepper to taste
- 20 oz. pineapple
- 2 tablespoons pineapple juice
- 4 burger buns

Method:

1. Add all ingredients except burger buns to your slow cooker.
2. Mix well.
3. Cover and cook on low for 8 hours.
4. Transfer pork to a cutting board.
5. Shred pork with a fork.
6. Preheat your Hamilton Dual Breakfast Sandwich Maker.
7. Wait for the green light to turn on.
8. Uncover the sandwich maker.
9. Add burger bottoms inside.
10. Top with pulled pork mixture.
11. Add burger bun tops.
12. Cover the sandwich maker.
13. Cook for 4 minutes.

Serving Suggestions:

Add lettuce to the sandwich.

Preparation & Cooking Tips:

You can also use whole wheat burger buns.

Italian Pulled Pork Sandwich

Preparation Time: 30 minutes
Cooking Time: 8 hours and 15 minutes
Servings: 4

Ingredients:

- 1 tablespoon olive oil
- 1 pork shoulder roast (boneless)
- 1 teaspoon cayenne pepper, optional
- 1 tablespoon steak seasoning
- 2 onions, thinly sliced
- 2 sweet red peppers, sliced
- ½ cup water
- 14 oz. canned diced tomatoes
- 4 burger buns

Method:

1. Combine all ingredients except burger buns to your slow cooker.
2. Seal the pot.
3. Cook on low for 8 hours.
4. Transfer pork to a cutting board.
5. Shred pork with a fork.
6. Put the shredded pork back to the slow cooker.
7. Cook for 10 minutes more.
8. Preheat your Hamilton Dual Breakfast Sandwich Maker.
9. Wait for the green light to turn on.
10. Open the sandwich maker.
11. Add burger bottoms inside.
12. Top with pulled pork mixture and tomato sauce.
13. Add burger bun tops.
14. Cover the sandwich maker.
15. Cook for 4 minutes.

Serving Suggestions:

Serve with fresh green salad.

Preparation & Cooking Tips:

You can also add cheese to the sandwich.

Tropical Ham Sandwich

Preparation Time: 5 minutes
Cooking Time: 4 minutes
Servings: 2

Ingredients:

- 4 whole wheat bread slices
- 2 deli ham slices
- 2 mozzarella cheese slices
- 2 pineapple rings

Method:

1.Preheat your Hamilton Dual Breakfast Sandwich Maker.
2.Wait for the green light to turn on.
3.Lift the lid.
4.Add bread slices inside.
5.Top with ham, cheese and pineapple.
6.Add remaining bread slices.
7.Cover the sandwich maker.
8.Cook for 4 minutes.

Serving Suggestions:

Serve with your favorite condiments.

Preparation & Cooking Tips:

Canned pineapple can be used if fresh pineapple is not available.

Maple Pork Sausage

Preparation Time: 10 minutes
Cooking Time: 4 minutes
Servings: 2

Ingredients:

- 2 burger buns
- 2 pork sausage, cooked and sliced
- 1 maple syrup
- ¼ cup caramelized onions

Method:

1. Toss pork sausage in maple syrup.
2. Preheat your Hamilton Dual Breakfast Sandwich Maker.
3. Wait for the green light to turn on.
4. Uncover the sandwich maker.
5. Add burger bun bottoms inside.
6. Top with sausage mixture and caramelized onions.
7. Add burger bun tops.
8. Cover the sandwich maker.
9. Cook for 4 minutes.

Serving Suggestions:

You can add lettuce and tomato to the sandwich if you like.

Preparation & Cooking Tips:

Use whole wheat burger buns.

CHAPTER 6:
FISH & SEAFOOD RECIPES

Crispy Fish Sandwich

Preparation Time: 5 minutes
Cooking Time: 10 minutes
Servings: 2

Ingredients:

- 4 frozen breaded fish strips
- Cooking spray
- 2 tablespoons mayonnaise
- 1 teaspoon sweet pickle relish
- 2 whole wheat burger buns, split in half
- 4 slices sweet onion

Method:

1. Spray fish strips with oil.
2. Cook in a pan over medium heat until golden and crispy.
3. Mix mayo and sweet pickle relish in a bowl.
4. Preheat your Hamilton Dual Breakfast Sandwich Maker.
5. Wait for the green light to turn on.
6. Open the sandwich maker.
7. Add burger bun bottoms inside.
8. Spread with mayo mixture.
9. Top with fish and onion.
10. Add burger bun tops.
11. Cover the sandwich maker.
12. Cook for 4 minutes.

Serving Suggestions:

Serve with tomato and cucumber salad.

Preparation & Cooking Tips:

You can also make your own breaded fish strips using cod fillet if you like.

Salsa Fish

Preparation Time: 10 minutes
Cooking Time: 4 minutes
Servings: 2

Ingredients:

- 4 whole wheat bread slices
- 2 cod fillets, grilled and sliced into strips
- 4 tablespoons salsa
- 1 teaspoon sweet pickle relish
- ½ teaspoon dried parsley flakes

Method:

1. Preheat your Hamilton Dual Breakfast Sandwich Maker.
2. Wait for the green light to turn on.
3. Lift the cover.
4. Add bread slices inside.
5. Top with fish, salsa and sweet pickle relish.
6. Sprinkle with parsley flakes.
7. Add remaining bread slices.
8. Cover the sandwich maker.
9. Cook for 4 minutes.

Serving Suggestions:

Season with salt and pepper.

Preparation & Cooking Tips:

You can also serve with avocado slices.

Fish & Tartar Sauce Sandwich

Preparation Time: 10 minutes
Cooking Time: 4 minutes
Servings: 2

Ingredients:

- 4 whole wheat bread slices
- 4 slices cucumber
- 2 breaded cod fillets, cooked
- 4 tablespoons tartar sauce

Method:

1. Preheat your Hamilton Dual Breakfast Sandwich Maker.
2. Wait for the green light to turn on.
3. Open the sandwich maker.
4. Add bread slices inside.
5. Top with cucumber and fish
6. Drizzle with tartar sauce.
7. Add remaining bread slices.
8. Cover the sandwich maker.
9. Cook for 4 minutes.

Serving Suggestions:

You can also add lettuce and tomato slices to the sandwich.

Preparation & Cooking Tips:

You can also use toasted rolls for this recipe.

Tuna Burgers

Preparation Time: 10 minutes
Cooking Time: 10 minutes
Servings: 4

Ingredients:

Patty
• 2 cups tuna flakes
• 1 egg, beaten
• ½ cup breadcrumbs
• 1 red onion, minced
• 1 tablespoon celery, chopped
Sandwich
• 8 whole wheat bread slices
• 4 tablespoons mayonnaise

Method:

1. Mix the patty ingredients in a bowl.
2. Form into patties.
3. Cook in a pan over medium heat for 2 to 3 minutes per side.
4. Preheat your Hamilton Dual Breakfast Sandwich Maker.
5. Wait for the green light to turn on.
6. Lift the lid.
7. Add bread slices inside.
8. Spread with mayo.
9. Top with tuna patties.
10. Add remaining bread slices.
11. Cover the sandwich maker.
12. Cook for 4 minutes.

Serving Suggestions:

Add lettuce leaves and tomatoes to the sandwich.

Preparation & Cooking Tips:

You can also add chopped parsley to the tuna burger.

Shrimp Salad Sandwich

Preparation Time: 10 minutes
Cooking Time: 4 minutes
Servings: 2

Ingredients:

- 1 cup shrimp, peeled, deveined, cooked and chopped
- 4 tablespoons mayonnaise
- 1 teaspoon lemon juice
- 1 tablespoon green onion, chopped
- 1 teaspoon Old Bay seasoning
- 2 burger buns, split

Method:

1. In a bowl, combine all the ingredients except burger buns.
2. Preheat your Hamilton Dual Breakfast Sandwich Maker.
3. Wait for the green light to turn on.
4. Open the sandwich maker.
5. Add burger bun bottoms inside.
6. Spread with shrimp mixture.
7. Add burger bun tops.
8. Seal the sandwich maker.
9. Cook for 4 minutes.

Serving Suggestions:

Add Romaine lettuce to the sandwich.

Preparation & Cooking Tips:

You can also use chopped crabmeat for this recipe.

Blackened Salmon Sandwich

Preparation Time: 10 minutes
Cooking Time: 12 minutes
Servings: 2

Ingredients:

- 2 salmon fillets
- 2 teaspoons blackening seasoning
- 4 whole bread slices
- 4 tablespoons mayonnaise
- 1 red onion, sliced thinly

Method:

1. Preheat your grill to medium.
2. Sprinkle salmon with blackening seasoning.
3. Grill salmon for 3 to 4 minutes per side.
4. Preheat your Hamilton Dual Breakfast Sandwich Maker.
5. Wait for the green light to turn on.
6. Open the sandwich maker.
7. Add bread slices inside.
8. Spread with mayonnaise.
9. Top with grilled salmon and onion slices.
10. Add remaining bread slices.
11. Close the sandwich maker.
12. Cook for 4 minutes.

Serving Suggestions:

Serve with guacamole.

Preparation & Cooking Tips:

You can also use other fish fillet such as cod for this recipe.

Salmon Salad Sandwich

Preparation Time: 5 minutes
Cooking Time: 4 minutes
Servings: 2

Ingredients:

- 1 cup salmon flakes
- ¼ cup cream cheese
- 1 tablespoon mayonnaise
- 1 tablespoon lemon juice
- 2 tablespoon celery, minced
- 2 tablespoons carrot, shredded
- 1 teaspoon dill weed
- Salt and pepper to taste
- 2 burger buns, split in half

Method:

1. Combine all the ingredients except burger buns.
2. Preheat your Hamilton Dual Breakfast Sandwich Maker.
3. Wait for the green light to turn on.
4. Uncover the sandwich maker.
5. Add burger bottoms inside.
6. Spread with salmon mixture.
7. Add burger tops.
8. Cover the sandwich maker.
9. Cook for 4 minutes.

Serving Suggestions:

You can add arugula or lettuce to the sandwich.

Preparation & Cooking Tips:

Tuna flakes can also be used for this recipe.

Tuna Cheese Melt Sandwich

Preparation Time: 5 minutes
Cooking Time: 4 minutes
Servings: 2

Ingredients:

- 1 cup tuna flakes
- 4 tablespoons mayonnaise
- 1 tablespoon celery, minced
- 1 tablespoon green onion, minced
- 2 burger buns, split
- 2 slices mozzarella cheese

Method:

1. Mix all ingredients except buns and cheese.
2. Preheat your Hamilton Dual Breakfast Sandwich Maker.
3. Once the green light turns on, lift the lid.
4. Add burger bottoms inside.
5. Spread with tuna mixture.
6. Top with cheese.
7. Add burger tops.
8. Cover the sandwich maker.
9. Cook for 4 minutes.

Serving Suggestions:

Add lettuce to the sandwich.

Preparation & Cooking Tips:

You can also add dried parsley or basil to the mixture.

Tuna & Tarragon Salad Sandwich

Preparation Time: 5 minutes
Cooking Time: 4 minutes
Servings: 2

Ingredients:

- 1 cup tuna flakes
- 4 tablespoons mayonnaise
- 1 tablespoon capers
- 1 teaspoon lime juice
- 1 teaspoon tarragon
- ¼ teaspoon lemon pepper seasoning
- 2 burger buns, split

Method:

1. Mix all ingredients except buns.
2. Preheat your Hamilton Dual Breakfast Sandwich Maker.
3. Once the green light turns on, lift the lid.
4. Add burger bottoms inside.
5. Top with tuna mixture.
6. Add burger tops.
7. Cover the sandwich maker.
8. Cook for 4 minutes.

Serving Suggestions:

Add coleslaw mixture to the sandwich.

Preparation & Cooking Tips:

Salmon flakes can also be used for this recipe.

Lemon Shrimp Sandwich

Preparation Time: 10 minutes
Cooking Time: 4 minutes
Servings: 2

Ingredients:

- 1 cup shrimp, peeled, deveined, cooked and chopped
- 4 tablespoons mayonnaise
- 1 teaspoon lemon juice
- 1 teaspoon dried dill
- 4 burger buns

Method:

1. Combine all ingredients except buns.
2. Preheat your Hamilton Dual Breakfast Sandwich Maker.
3. When the green light turns on, lift the lid.
4. Add burger bottoms inside.
5. Spread with shrimp mixture.
6. Add burger tops.
7. Cover the sandwich maker.
8. Cook for 4 minutes.

Serving Suggestions:

Add lettuce and tomato slices to the sandwich.

Preparation & Cooking Tips:

You can also add other herbs to the shrimp mixture.

CHAPTER 7:
VEGAN SANDWICH RECIPES

Hummus & Avocado Sandwich

Preparation Time: 5 minutes
Cooking Time: 4 minutes
Servings: 2

Ingredients:

- 4 vegan bread slices
- ½ cup mashed avocado
- ¼ cup hummus
- 4 slices cucumber

Method:

1. Preheat your Hamilton Dual Breakfast Sandwich Maker.
2. When the green light turns on, lift the lid.
3. Add vegan bread slices inside.
4. Spread with mashed avocado and hummus.
5. Top with cucumber.
6. Add remaining bread slices.
7. Close the sandwich maker.
8. Cook for 4 minutes.

Serving Suggestions:

Serve with additional hummus.

Preparation & Cooking Tips:

You can also add sprouts to the sandwich.

Avocado & Cilantro Sandwich

Preparation Time: 5 minutes
Cooking Time: 4 minutes
Servings: 2

Ingredients:

- 4 vegan bread slices
- ¼ cup mashed avocado
- ¼ cup cilantro, chopped
- 1 tomato, sliced

Method:

1. Preheat your Hamilton Dual Breakfast Sandwich Maker.
2. Wait for the green light to turn on, lift the lid.
3. Add vegan bread slices inside.
4. Spread with mashed avocado
5. Top with cilantro and tomato.
6. Add remaining bread slices.
7. Close the sandwich maker.
8. Cook for 4 minutes.

Serving Suggestions:

Season with a little salt and pepper.

Preparation & Cooking Tips:

You can also add other vegetables to the sandwich like shredded carrots.

Vegan Bacon Sandwich

Preparation Time: 10 minutes
Cooking Time: 4 minutes
Servings: 2

Ingredients:

- 4 vegan bread slices
- 2 tablespoons vegan mayo
- 1 tomato, sliced
- 4 slices vegan bacon, cooked

Method:

1. Preheat your Hamilton Dual Breakfast Sandwich Maker.
2. Wait for the green light to turn on
3. Open the sandwich maker.
4. Add vegan bread slices inside.
5. Spread with vegan mayo.
6. Top with tomato slices and bacon.
7. Add remaining bread slices.
8. Close the sandwich maker.
9. Cook for 4 minutes.

Serving Suggestions:

You can also add cucumber slices and lettuce to the sandwich.

Preparation & Cooking Tips:

If you'd like to add cheese, there are also vegan cheese that you can use for this recipe.

Tempeh Sandwich

Preparation Time: 10 minutes
Cooking Time: 4 minutes
Servings: 2

Ingredients:

- 4 vegan bread slices
- 4 tempeh slices, fried
- 1 cup arugula
- ½ cup sun-dried tomatoes
- 4 tablespoons vegan mayo

Method:

1. Preheat your Hamilton Dual Breakfast Sandwich Maker.
2. Wait for the green light to turn on
3. Uncover the sandwich maker.
4. Add vegan bread slices inside.
5. Spread with vegan mayo.
6. Top with tempeh, arugula and sun-dried tomato slices.
7. Add remaining bread slices.
8. Seal the sandwich maker.
9. Cook for 4 minutes.

Serving Suggestions:

Serve with avocado slices.

Preparation & Cooking Tips:

Fresh tomato can also be used if sun-dried tomato is not available.

Chickpea Sandwich

Preparation Time: 5 minutes
Cooking Time: 2 minutes
Servings: 2

Ingredients:

- 4 vegan bread slices
- ½ cup chickpeas, rinsed, drained and mashed
- ½ red onion, minced
- 1 tablespoon celery, minced
- ¼ cup vegan mayo
- 1 teaspoon lemon juice
- 1 teaspoon kelp flakes
- 1 tablespoon parsley

Method:

1. Combine all ingredients except bread.
2. Preheat your Hamilton Dual Breakfast Sandwich Maker.
3. Wait for the green light to turn on
4. Open the sandwich maker.
5. Add vegan bread slices inside.
6. Spread with chickpea mixture.
7. Add remaining bread slices.
8. Seal the sandwich maker.
9. Cook for 2 minutes.

Serving Suggestions:

Serve with tomato and cucumber salad.

Preparation & Cooking Tips:

Use freshly squeezed lemon juice.

Chickpea Curry Salad Sandwich

Preparation Time: 5 minutes
Cooking Time: 2 minutes
Servings: 2

Ingredients:

- 4 vegan bread slices
- 4 tablespoons vegan mayo
- 1 tablespoon Dijon mustard
- 1 cup chickpeas, rinsed and drained
- 1 teaspoon lemon juice
- 1 clove garlic, minced
- 2 teaspoons curry powder

Method:

1. In a bowl, mix all the ingredients except bread.
2. Preheat your Hamilton Dual Breakfast Sandwich Maker.
3. Wait for the green light to turn on.
4. Lift the lid up.
5. Add vegan bread slices inside.
6. Spread with chickpea salad mixture.
7. Add remaining bread slices.
8. Close the lid.
9. Cook for 2 minutes.

Serving Suggestions:

Add spinach and alfalfa sprouts to the sandwich.

Preparation & Cooking Tips:

Season chickpea salad with a little salt and pepper.

Tofu Sandwich

Preparation Time: 5 minutes
Cooking Time: 4 minutes
Servings: 2

Ingredients:

- 4 slices vegan bread
- 2 tablespoons vegan mayo
- 2 slices tofu, fried
- 4 slices cucumber
- 4 slices tomato

Method:

1. Preheat your Hamilton Dual Breakfast Sandwich Maker.
2. Wait for the green light to turn on.
3. Open the sandwich maker.
4. Spread with mayo.
5. Add vegan bread slices inside.
6. Top with tofu, cucumber and tomato.
7. Add remaining bread slices.
8. Cover and cook for 4 minutes.

Serving Suggestions:

Serve with your favorite condiments.

Preparation & Cooking Tips:

Use firm tofu for this recipe.

Vegan Meatballs Sandwich

Preparation Time: 10 minutes
Cooking Time: 4 minutes
Servings: 2

Ingredients:

- 2 vegan burger buns
- 8 vegan meatballs, cooked
- Vegan cream sauce
- Vegan cheese sauce

Method:

1. Preheat your Hamilton Dual Breakfast Sandwich Maker.
2. Once the green light is on, lift the lid.
3. Add vegan bread slices inside.
4. Top with meatballs.
5. Drizzle with cream sauce and cheese sauce.
6. Add remaining bread slices.
7. Cover and cook for 4 minutes.

Serving Suggestions:

Serve with favorite vegetable side dish.

Preparation & Cooking Tips:

You can also make your own vegan meatballs using crumbled tofu.

Tofu Salad Sandwich

Preparation Time: 5 minutes
Cooking Time: 2 minutes
Servings: 2

Ingredients:

- 4 vegan bread slices
- 1 cup tofu cubes, sliced and cooked
- 2 tablespoons vegan mayo
- 1 tablespoon mustard
- 1 tablespoon sweet relish
- ¼ red onion, minced
- 1 teaspoon lemon juice
- 1 teaspoon parsley, chopped
- Salt and pepper to taste

Method:

1. In a bowl, combine all the ingredients except bread.
2. Preheat your Hamilton Dual Breakfast Sandwich Maker.
3. Once the green light is on, open the sandwich maker.
4. Add vegan bread slices inside.
5. Top with tofu mixture.
6. Add remaining bread slices.
7. Cover and cook for 2 minutes.

Serving Suggestions:

Add Romaine lettuce to the sandwich.

Preparation & Cooking Tips:

Use freshly squeezed lemon juice.

Buffalo Tofu Sandwich

Preparation Time: 10 minutes
Cooking Time: 4 minutes
Servings: 2

Ingredients:

- 4 vegan bread slices
- 1 cup tofu, cubed and fried
- ¼ cup Buffalo sauce
- ¼ cup caramelized onions

Method:

1. Toss tofu cubes in Buffalo sauce.
2. Preheat your Hamilton Dual Breakfast Sandwich Maker.
3. Wait for the green light to turn on.
4. Open the sandwich maker.
5. Add vegan bread slices inside.
6. Top with tofu mixture and onions.
7. Add remaining bread slices.
8. Cover and cook for 4 minutes.

Serving Suggestions:

You can also add lettuce carrot strips to the sandwich.

Preparation & Cooking Tips:

Use vegan Buffalo sauce.

CHAPTER 8:
VEGETARIAN SANDWICH RECIPES

Raddish & Cheese Sandwich

Preparation Time: 5 minutes
Cooking Time: 4 minutes
Servings: 2

Ingredients:

- 4 slices whole wheat bread
- ¼ cup mashed avocado
- 4 slices cheddar cheese
- 1 radish, sliced thinly
- 1 cup spinach

Method:

1. Preheat your Hamilton Dual Breakfast Sandwich Maker.
2. Wait for the green light to turn on.
3. Lift the cover.
4. Add bread slices inside.
5. Spread with mashed avocado.
6. Top with cheese, radish and spinach.
7. Add remaining bread slices.
8. Cover and cook for 4 minutes.

Serving Suggestions:

Serve with favorite condiments.

Preparation & Cooking Tips:

You can also use Provolone cheese for this recipe.

Tomato, Cheese & Pesto Sandwich

Preparation Time: 5 minutes
Cooking Time: 4 minutes
Servings: 2

Ingredients:

- 4 slices whole wheat bread
- 2 tablespoons mayonnaise
- 2 tablespoons basil pesto
- 1 tomato, sliced
- 2 slices mozzarella cheese

Method:

1. Preheat your Hamilton Dual Breakfast Sandwich Maker.
2. When the green light is on, open the sandwich maker
3. Place bread slices inside.
4. Spread with a mix of mayo and pesto.
5. Top with tomato and cheese.
6. Add remaining bread slices.
7. Seal the sandwich maker.
8. Cook for 4 minutes.

Serving Suggestions:

Serve with additional pesto sauce.

Preparation & Cooking Tips:

You can also make your own pesto sauce if you like.

Greek Veggie Sandwich

Preparation Time: 5 minutes
Cooking Time: 4 minutes
Servings: 2

Ingredients:

- 4 slices whole wheat bread
- 2 slices mozzarella cheese
- ¼ cup sun-dried tomatoes, chopped
- 2 tablespoons olives, chopped
- 2 teaspoons capers, chopped
- ¼ cup basil, chopped

Method:

1. Preheat your Hamilton Dual Breakfast Sandwich Maker.
2. Once the green light is on, open the cover.
3. Put bread slices inside.
4. Mix the remaining ingredients in a bowl.
5. Add the mixture on top of the cheese.
6. Top with remaining bread slices.
7. Close the sandwich maker.
8. Cook for 4 minutes.

Serving Suggestions:

Serve with fresh green salad.

Preparation & Cooking Tips:

You can also add chopped oregano to the mixture.

Lentil & Ricotta Sandwich

Preparation Time: 5 minutes
Cooking Time: 4 minutes
Servings: 2

Ingredients:

- ¼ cup ricotta cheese
- 1 tablespoons fresh dill, chopped
- 1 tablespoon green onion, chopped
- 1/8 cup walnuts, chopped
- 4 whole wheat bread slices
- ½ cup cooked green lentils

Method:

1. Combine ricotta cheese, dill, green onion and walnuts in a bowl.
2. Preheat your Hamilton Dual Breakfast Sandwich Maker.
3. Wait for the green light to turn on.
4. Open the cover.
5. Place bread slices inside.
6. Spread ricotta cheese mixture on the bread slices.
7. Top with lentils.
8. Add remaining bread slices.
9. Close the sandwich maker.
10. Cook for 4 minutes.

Serving Suggestions:

Serve with fresh fruit juice.

Preparation & Cooking Tips:

Cottage cheese can also be used in place of ricotta cheese.

Onion & Mushroom Sandwich

Preparation Time: 5 minutes
Cooking Time: 7 minutes
Servings: 2

Ingredients:

- 1 teaspoon butter
- 1 red onion, sliced thinly
- 1 clove garlic, minced
- ½ cup mushrooms
- 4 slices rye bread
- 2 tablespoons mayonnaise
- 2 cheddar cheese slices

Method:

1. Add butter to a pan over medium heat.
2. Cook onion, garlic and mushrooms for 2 to 3 minutes, stirring often.
3. Transfer to a plate.
4. Preheat your Hamilton Dual Breakfast Sandwich Maker.
5. Wait for the green light to turn on.
6. Open the sandwich maker.
7. Add bread slices inside.
8. Spread with mayo.
9. Top with onion mixture.
10. Add remaining bread slices.
11. Seal the sandwich maker.
12. Cook for 4 minutes.

Serving Suggestions:

Serve with potato fries.

Preparation & Cooking Tips:

Use cremini mushrooms if available.

Avocado Egg Salad Sandwich

Preparation Time: 10 minutes
Cooking Time: 4 minutes
Servings: 2

Ingredients:

- ¼ cup plain Greek yogurt
- 4 hard boiled eggs, peeled and mashed
- 1 ripe avocado, mashed
- 1 teaspoon lemon juice
- 2 tablespoons walnuts, crushed
- Salt and pepper to taste
- 4 whole wheat bread slices

Method:

1. Mix the yogurt, eggs, avocado, lemon juice, walnuts, salt and pepper in a bowl.
2. Preheat your Hamilton Dual Breakfast Sandwich Maker.
3. Wait for the green light to turn on.
4. Lift the cover.
5. Add bread slices inside.
6. Spread with egg salad mixture.
7. Add remaining bread slices.
8. Seal the sandwich maker.
9. Cook for 4 minutes.

Serving Suggestions:

Add lettuce and tomato slices to the sandwich before serving.

Preparation & Cooking Tips:

You can also add chopped parsley to the mixture.

Hummus & Spinach Sandwich

Preparation Time: 5 minutes
Cooking Time: 4 minutes
Servings: 2

Ingredients:

- 4 slices cucumber
- 4 slices tomato
- 4 tablespoons feta cheese
- 1 teaspoon lemon juice
- 1 tablespoon olive oil
- 4 tablespoons hummus
- 1 cup spinach
- 4 whole wheat bread slices

Method:

1. Toss cucumber, tomato and feta cheese in lemon juice and olive oil.
2. Preheat your Hamilton Dual Breakfast Sandwich Maker.
3. Wait for the green light to turn on.
4. Open the sandwich maker
5. Place bread slices inside.
6. Spread with hummus.
7. Top with cucumber mixture.
8. Add remaining bread slices.
9. Seal the sandwich maker.
10. Cook for 4 minutes.

Serving Suggestions:

Serve with your favorite fruit juice.

Preparation & Cooking Tips:

You can also season cucumber mixture with dried oregano and dill.

Jalapeños & Feta Cheese Sandwich

Preparation Time: 5 minutes
Cooking Time: 4 minutes
Servings: 2

Ingredients:

- 2 jalapeños, chopped
- ½ cup feta cheese, crumbled
- 4 slices sourdough bread
- 3 tablespoons olive tapenade

Method:

1.Combine jalapeños and feta cheese in a bowl.
2.Preheat your Hamilton Dual Breakfast Sandwich Maker.
3.Once the green light is on, open the cover.
4.Put bread slices inside.
5.Spread with olive tapenade.
6.Top with feta cheese mixture.
7.Add remaining bread slices.
8.Seal the sandwich maker.
9.Cook for 4 minutes.

Serving Suggestions:

Serve with additional crumbled feta cheese.

Preparation & Cooking Tips:

You can also use sweet pepper for this recipe.

Crispy Tofu Sandwich

Preparation Time: 10 minutes
Cooking Time: 4 minutes
Servings: 2

Ingredients:

- 4 slices whole wheat bread
- 4 tablespoons mayonnaise
- 4 slices tofu, fried crispy
- 2 slices cheddar cheese
- 4 slices tomato

Method:

1. Preheat your Hamilton Dual Breakfast Sandwich Maker.
2. When the green light is on, open the cover.
3. Add bread slices inside.
4. Spread with mayo.
5. Top with tofu, cheese and tomato.
6. Add remaining bread slices.
7. Seal the sandwich maker.
8. Cook for 4 minutes.

Serving Suggestions:

Serve with sweet chili sauce.

Preparation & Cooking Tips:

Use low fat mayo.

Turmeric Chickpea Sandwich

Preparation Time: 5 minutes
Cooking Time: 4 minutes
Servings: 2

Ingredients:

- 4 slices whole wheat bread
- 4 tablespoons mayo
- 1 cup chickpeas, cooked and mashed
- 1 clove garlic, minced
- 1 teaspoon ground turmeric
- Salt and pepper to taste

Method:

1. Preheat your Hamilton Dual Breakfast Sandwich Maker.
2. When the green light is on, open the sandwich maker.
3. Place bread slices inside.
4. Mix remaining ingredients in a bowl.
5. Top bread slices with the mixture.
6. Add remaining bread slices.
7. Close the sandwich maker.
8. Cook for 4 minutes.

Serving Suggestions:

Add avocado slices to the sandwich before serving.

Preparation & Cooking Tips:

You can also add chopped parsley to the chickpea mixture.

CHAPTER 9:
CHEESE SANDWICH RECIPES

Cheese & Pimiento Sandwich

Preparation Time: 5 minutes
Cooking Time: 4 minutes
Servings: 2

Ingredients:

- 4 slices sourdough bread
- 4 tablespoons butter
- ¼ cup pimiento cheese spread
- 2 slices cheddar cheese

Method:

1. Preheat your Hamilton Dual Breakfast Sandwich Maker.
2. Once the green light is on, open the sandwich maker.
3. Add bread slices inside.
4. Spread with butter and cheese spread.
5. Top with cheddar slices.
6. Add remaining bread slices.
7. Close the sandwich maker.
8. Cook for 4 minutes.

Serving Suggestions:

You can also add lettuce before serving.

Preparation & Cooking Tips:

Whole wheat bread can also be used in place of sourdough bread.

Cheese & Avocado Sandwich

Preparation Time: 5 minutes
Cooking Time: 4 minutes
Servings: 2

Ingredients:

- 4 slices sourdough bread
- ¼ cup mashed avocado
- ¼ cup Gruyere cheese, shredded
- 2 slices sharp white cheddar cheese

Method:

1. Preheat your Hamilton Dual Breakfast Sandwich Maker.
2. When the green light is on, lift the cover.
3. Put bread slices inside.
4. Spread mashed avocado on top of bread slices.
5. Sprinkle with Gruyere cheese.
6. Top with cheddar slices.
7. Add remaining bread slices.
8. Seal the sandwich maker.
9. Cook for 4 minutes.

Serving Suggestions:

Serve with fresh green salad.

Preparation & Cooking Tips:

You can also use Parmesan cheese instead of Gruyere cheese.

Cheese & Mushroom Sandwich

Preparation Time: 5 minutes
Cooking Time: 10 minutes
Servings: 2

Ingredients:

- 2 tablespoons butter
- 1 clove garlic, minced
- 4 Portobello mushroom caps
- Salt and pepper to taste
- 4 slices sourdough bread
- 3 tablespoons mayonnaise
- 3 tablespoons Manchego, shredded
- 4 slices sharp white cheddar cheese

Method:

1. Add butter to a pan over medium heat.
2. Cook the garlic for 30 seconds.
3. Add the mushroom caps.
4. Season with salt and pepper.
5. Preheat your Hamilton Dual Breakfast Sandwich Maker.
6. When the green light is on, lift the cover.
7. Add bread slices inside.
8. Spread with mayo.
9. Sprinkle with Manchego cheese.
10. Top with mushrooms and cheddar slices.
11. Add remaining bread slices.
12. Seal the sandwich maker.
13. Cook for 4 minutes.

Serving Suggestions:

Add caramelized onions to the sandwich.

Preparation & Cooking Tips:

Rinse mushroom caps thoroughly and remove gills and stems.

Cheese & Pickled Onion Sandwich

Preparation Time: 5 minutes
Cooking Time: 4 minutes
Servings: 2

Ingredients:

- 4 slices sourdough bread
- 4 tablespoons butter
- ¼ cup pickled pearl onions, sliced in half
- 4 slices Brie cheese

Method:

1. Preheat your Hamilton Dual Breakfast Sandwich Maker.
2. When the green light is on, lift the cover.
3. Add bread slices inside.
4. Spread with butter.
5. Top with onions and Brie slices.
6. Place remaining bread slices.
7. Close the sandwich maker.
8. Cook for 4 minutes.

Serving Suggestions:

Serve with your favorite smoothie.

Preparation & Cooking Tips:

You can also use other pickles for this recipe.

Cheese & Date Sandwich

Preparation Time: 5 minutes
Cooking Time: 4 minutes
Servings: 2

Ingredients:

- 4 slices sourdough bread
- 2 tablespoons butter
- 4 dates, pitted and chopped
- ¼ cup feta cheese

Method:

1. Preheat your Hamilton Dual Breakfast Sandwich Maker.
2. Once the green light is on, open the sandwich maker.
3. Put bread slices inside.
4. Spread with butter.
5. Top with dates and feta cheese
6. Add remaining bread slices.
7. Put the cover down.
8. Cook for 4 minutes.

Serving Suggestions:

Serve with additional butter and date jam.

Preparation & Cooking Tips:

You can also use other soft cheese for this recipe.

Tomato, Basil & Cheese Sandwich

Preparation Time: 15 minutes
Cooking Time: 4 minutes
Servings: 2

Ingredients:

- 2 tablespoons olive oil
- ¼ teaspoon garlic powder
- 3 tablespoons Parmesan cheese, grated
- 4 slices tomatoes
- 2 tablespoons fresh basil, minced
- 2 teaspoons balsamic vinegar
- Salt and pepper to taste
- 4 slices Italian bread
- 2 slices mozzarella cheese

Method:

1. Mix olive oil, garlic powder and Parmesan cheese in a bowl.
2. Brush both sides of bread with this mixture.
3. In another bowl, combine the tomatoes, basil, vinegar, salt and pepper.
4. Preheat your Hamilton Dual Breakfast Sandwich Maker.
5. Once the green light is on, open the sandwich maker.
6. Add bread slices inside.
7. Top with tomato mixture and mozzarella cheese.
8. Add remaining bread slices.
9. Close the cover.
10. Cook for 4 minutes.

Serving Suggestions:

Serve with fresh green salad.

Preparation & Cooking Tips:

You can also add olives to the mixture.

Cheese & Apricot Sandwich

Preparation Time: 5 minutes
Cooking Time: 4 minutes
Servings: 2

Ingredients:

- 4 slices sourdough bread
- 2 tablespoons butter
- 4 tablespoons apricot preserves
- 2 slices sharp white cheddar cheese

Method:

1. Preheat your Hamilton Dual Breakfast Sandwich Maker.
2. Wait for the green light to turn on.
3. Open the sandwich maker.
4. Add bread slices inside.
5. Spread with butter.
6. Top with apricot preserves and cheddar cheese.
7. Add remaining bread slices.
8. Seal and cook for 4 minutes.

Serving Suggestions:

Serve with additional apricot preserves.

Preparation & Cooking Tips:

Whole wheat bread slices can also be used for this recipe.

Cheese & Bacon Sandwich

Preparation Time: 5 minutes
Cooking Time: 4 minutes
Servings: 2

Ingredients:

- 4 slices sourdough bread
- 2 tablespoons butter
- ¼ cup Gruyere cheese, shredded
- 4 slices bacon, cooked crisp
- 4 slices sun-dried tomatoes
- 2 slices cheddar cheese

Method:

1. Preheat your Hamilton Dual Breakfast Sandwich Maker.
2. Wait for the green light to turn on.
3. Lift the cover.
4. Put bread slices inside.
5. Spread with butter.
6. Sprinkle with Gruyere cheese.
7. Top with the bacon, tomato and cheddar.
8. Add remaining bread slices.
9. Seal and cook for 4 minutes.

Serving Suggestions:

Serve with hot pepper sauce.

Preparation & Cooking Tips:

Deli ham can also be used in place of bacon.

Cheese & Blueberry Jam Sandwich

Preparation Time: 5 minutes
Cooking Time: 4 minutes
Servings: 2

Ingredients:

- 4 slices sourdough bread
- 4 tablespoons blueberry jam
- ¼ cup Monterey Jack cheese, shredded
- 2 slices cheddar cheese

Method:

1. Preheat your Hamilton Dual Breakfast Sandwich Maker.
2. Wait for the green light to turn on.
3. Lift the cover.
4. Add bread slices inside.
5. Spread with blueberry jam.
6. Sprinkle with Monterey Jack cheese.
7. Top with cheddar slices.
8. Add remaining bread slices.
9. Cover and cook for 4 minutes.

Serving Suggestions:

Serve with fresh blueberries.

Preparation & Cooking Tips:

Gruyere cheese can be used in place of Monterey Jack cheese.

Cheese & Pepperoni Sandwich

Preparation Time: 5 minutes
Cooking Time: 4 minutes
Servings: 2

Ingredients:

- 4 slices sourdough bread
- 2 tablespoons butter
- ¼ cup pepperoni slices
- ½ cup Gruyere cheese, shredded
- ¼ cup cheddar cheese, shredded

Method:

1. Preheat your Hamilton Dual Breakfast Sandwich Maker.
2. Wait for the green light to turn on.
3. Open the sandwich maker.
4. Place bread slices inside.
5. Spread with butter.
6. Top with pepperoni, Gruyere and cheddar cheese.
7. Add remaining bread slices.
8. Cover and cook for 4 minutes.

Serving Suggestions:

Serve with fresh green salad.

Preparation & Cooking Tips:

If sourdough bread is not available, you can also use rye bread for this recipe.

CHAPTER 10: TEA SANDWICHES

Cucumber Party Sandwiches

Preparation Time: 5 minutes
Cooking Time: 4 minutes
Servings: 6

Ingredients:

- 8 oz. cream cheese
- 2 tablespoons mayonnaise
- 2 teaspoons Italian salad dressing mix
- 12 slices rye bread
- 24 slices cucumber

Method:

1. Mix cream cheese, mayo and Italian salad dressing mix.
2. Preheat your Hamilton Dual Breakfast Sandwich Maker.
3. Wait for the green light to turn on.
4. Open the sandwich maker.
5. Add rye bread slices inside.
6. Spread with mayo mixture.
7. Top with cucumber slices.
8. Add remaining bread slices.
9. Cover and cook for 4 minutes.
10. Slice each sandwich into 4.

Serving Suggestions:

Serve with slivered pickled onions.

Preparation & Cooking Tips:

You can also add dried dill to the sandwich.

Roast Beef Mini Sandwiches

Preparation Time: 5 minutes
Cooking Time: 4 minutes
Servings: 6

Ingredients:

- 12 slices rye bread
- ¼ cup mayonnaise
- 2 tablespoons mustard
- 6 slices cooked roast beef

Method:

1. Preheat your Hamilton Dual Breakfast Sandwich Maker.
2. Once the green light is on, open the sandwich maker.
3. Add rye bread slices inside.
4. Spread with mayo and mustard.
5. Top with roast beef.
6. Add remaining bread slices.
7. Cover the sandwich maker.
8. Cook for 4 minutes.
9. Slice each sandwich into 4.

Serving Suggestions:

Secure the mini sandwiches with toothpicks.

Preparation & Cooking Tips:

Use Dijon style mustard.

Chicken Salad Mini Sandwiches

Preparation Time: 5 minutes
Cooking Time: 4 minutes
Servings: 6

Ingredients:

- 12 slices rye bread
- ½ cup mayonnaise
- 2 cups chicken breast, cooked and shredded
- 2 green onions, chopped
- ½ cup dried cranberries, chopped
- ¼ cup sweet pickles, chopped
- Salt and pepper to taste

Method:

1. Preheat your Hamilton Dual Breakfast Sandwich Maker.
2. Wait for the green light to turn on.
3. Open the sandwich maker.
4. Add rye bread slices inside.
5. Mix the remaining ingredients in a bowl.
6. Top the bread with the chicken salad mixture.
7. Add remaining bread slices.
8. Cover the sandwich maker.
9. Cook for 4 minutes.
10. Slice each sandwich into 4.

Serving Suggestions:

Add lettuce to the sandwich.

Preparation & Cooking Tips:

You can also add curry powder to the mixture.

Ham & Cheese Party Sandwiches

Preparation Time: 5 minutes
Cooking Time: 4 minutes
Servings: 6

Ingredients:

- 12 slices rye bread
- ½ cup mayonnaise
- 6 slices deli ham
- 6 slices cheddar cheese

Method:

1. Preheat your Hamilton Dual Breakfast Sandwich Maker.
2. Wait for the green light to turn on.
3. Open the sandwich maker.
4. Add rye bread slices inside.
5. Spread with mayo.
6. Top with the ham and cheddar cheese.
7. Add remaining bread slices.
8. Cover the sandwich maker.
9. Cook for 4 minutes.
10. Slice each sandwich into 4.

Serving Suggestions:

Thread olives into the sandwiches.

Preparation & Cooking Tips:

You can also use turkey or chicken ham.

Crab Salad Tea Sandwiches

Preparation Time: 5 minutes
Cooking Time: 4 minutes
Servings: 6

Ingredients:

- 12 slices rye bread
- ½ cup mayonnaise
- 1 cup crab meat, chopped
- 1 teaspoon lemon juice
- 2 green onions, minced
- Salt and pepper to taste

Method:

1. Preheat your Hamilton Dual Breakfast Sandwich Maker.
2. Once the green light is on, open the sandwich maker.
3. Add rye bread slices inside.
4. Mix the remaining ingredients in a bowl.
5. Top bread with the crab salad mixture.
6. Add remaining bread slices.
7. Seal the sandwich maker.
8. Cook for 4 minutes.
9. Slice each sandwich into 4.

Serving Suggestions:

Serve with cucumber and tomato salad.

Preparation & Cooking Tips:

You can also season with paprika.

Beef & Blue Cheese Tea Sandwiches

Preparation Time: 5 minutes
Cooking Time: 4 minutes
Servings: 6

Ingredients:

- 12 slices rye bread
- ½ cup mayonnaise
- 6 roast beef slices
- ½ cup blue cheese, crumbled

Method:

1. Preheat your Hamilton Dual Breakfast Sandwich Maker.
2. When the green light is on, open the sandwich maker.
3. Add rye bread slices inside.
4. Spread with mayo.
5. Top with roast beef and blue cheese.
6. Add remaining bread slices.
7. Close the sandwich maker.
8. Cook for 4 minutes.
9. Slice each sandwich into 4.

Serving Suggestions:

Add lettuce and tomatoes to the sandwich.

Preparation & Cooking Tips:

Cream cheese can also be used in place of blue cheese.

Avocado Tea Sandwich

Preparation Time: 5 minutes
Cooking Time: 4 minutes
Servings: 6

Ingredients:

- 12 slices rye bread
- 1 cup mashed avocado
- Salt and pepper to taste

Method:

1. Preheat your Hamilton Dual Breakfast Sandwich Maker.
2. Wait for the green light to turn on.
3. Open the sandwich maker.
4. Add rye bread slices inside.
5. Spread with mashed avocado.
6. Sprinkle with salt and pepper.
7. Add remaining bread slices.
8. Close the sandwich maker.
9. Cook for 4 minutes.
10. Slice each sandwich into 4.

Serving Suggestions:

Serve with additional avocado slices.

Preparation & Cooking Tips:

Use ripe avocado for this recipe.

Roast Beef & Sweet Pepper Sandwich

Preparation Time: 5 minutes
Cooking Time: 4 minutes
Servings: 6

Ingredients:

- 12 slices rye bread
- ½ cup mayo
- 3 red bell pepper, sliced into strips
- 6 slices deli roast beef
- ¼ cup Manchego cheese, shredded

Method:

1. Preheat your Hamilton Dual Breakfast Sandwich Maker.
2. Wait for the green light to turn on.
3. Open the sandwich maker.
4. Place rye bread slices inside.
5. Spread with mayo.
6. Top with bell pepper strips, beef slices and shredded cheese.
7. Add remaining bread slices.
8. Seal the sandwich maker.
9. Cook for 4 minutes.
10. Slice each sandwich into 4.

Serving Suggestions:

Serve with sweet potato fries.

Preparation & Cooking Tips:

Use Monterey Jack cheese if Manchego cheese is not available.

Bacon & Cheese Tea Sandwich

Preparation Time: 5 minutes
Cooking Time: 4 minutes
Servings: 6

Ingredients:

- ½ cup mayonnaise
- 1 green onion, chopped
- 12 slices whole wheat bread
- 6 slices bacon, cooked crispy
- 2 cups Monterey Jack cheese, shredded

Method:

1. Mix mayo and green onion in a bowl.
2. Preheat your Hamilton Dual Breakfast Sandwich Maker.
3. Wait for the green light to turn on.
4. Open the sandwich maker.
5. Place whole wheat bread slices inside.
6. Spread with mayo mixture.
7. Top with bacon and shredded cheese.
8. Add remaining bread slices.
9. Seal the sandwich maker.
10. Cook for 4 minutes.
11. Slice each sandwich into 4.

Serving Suggestions:

Serve with hot pepper sauce.

Preparation & Cooking Tips:

You can also use turkey bacon if you like.

Chicken & Cucumber Sandwich

Preparation Time: 5 minutes
Cooking Time: 4 minutes
Servings: 6

Ingredients:

• 6 chicken breast fillets
• 1 tablespoon olive oil
• 1 teaspoon dried tarragon
• 1 teaspoon dried oregano
• Salt and pepper to taste
• 12 slices rye bread
• ½ cup mayonnaise
• ½ cucumber, sliced thinly

Method:

1. Preheat your grill to medium.
2. Drizzle chicken breast fillet with olive oil.
3. Season with herbs, salt and pepper.
4. Preheat your Hamilton Dual Breakfast Sandwich Maker.
5. Wait for the green light to turn on.
6. Open the sandwich maker.
7. Place rye bread slices inside.
8. Spread with mayo.
9. Top with cucumber and grilled chicken.
10. Add remaining bread slices.
11. Close the sandwich maker.
12. Cook for 4 minutes.
13. Slice each sandwich into 4.

Serving Suggestions:

Serve with fresh green salad.

Preparation & Cooking Tips:

Use reduced-fat mayo to tone down calories and fat content.

CONCLUSION

As you can see, there are many wonderful things that this sandwich maker can do for you.

It will not only help you create delicious custom sandwiches that will satisfy your family and impress your guests, it will also help you reduce time and effort spent inside the kitchen.

This is a great deal, since things can get quite hectic during the week. And you don't need a kitchen appliance that will complicate things or make things harder for you. You need one that will work for you, one that will help you make the most out of your time.

And this is what the Hamilton Beach Dual Sandwich Maker can do for you.

happy cooking

APPENDIX RECIPE INDEX

Made in the USA
Columbia, SC
21 December 2024

50315332R00070